AIRCRAFT AND AEROSPACE MANUFACTURING

IN NORTHERN IRELAND

An Illustrated History – 1909 to the Present Day

GUY WARNER & ERNIE CROMIE

To Noel

With congratulations and
very best wishes on your 90ᵗʰ Birthday

Ernie Cromie

COLOURPOINT BOOKS

Published 2014 by Colourpoint Books
An imprint of Colourpoint Creative Ltd
Colourpoint House, Jubilee Business Park
Jubilee Road, Newtownards, BT23 4YH
Tel: 028 9182 6339
Fax: 028 9182 1900
E-mail: info@colourpoint.co.uk
Web: www.colourpoint.co.uk

First Edition
First Impression

Designed by April Sky Design, Newtownards
Tel: 028 9182 7195 • Web: www.aprilsky.co.uk

Printed by GPS Colour Graphics Ltd, Belfast

ISBN 978-1-78073-060-8

Front cover: A Short 360 and a 330 in formation. *(Bombardier Belfast)*
Small images (l-r): A later version of the Ferguson monoplane. *(Bombardier Belfast)*
A Solent 4 of Tasman Empire Airways. *(Bombardier Belfast)*
The Short SC.1 demonstrates transition from vertical to forward flight at RAE Bedford in 1960. *(Bombardier Belfast)*
Rear cover: Miles Messenger at Newtownards airfield. *(Miles Aircraft Collection)*
The manufacture of the Bombardier CRJ700's engine nacelles is carried out in Belfast. *(Bombardier Belfast)*
The launch of a Short Seacat missile. *(Bombardier Belfast)*

CONTENTS

ABOUT THE AUTHORS

Guy in 1958.

Guy Warner is a retired schoolteacher and former civil servant, who grew up in Newtownabbey, attending Abbots Cross Primary School and Belfast High School before going to Leicester University and later Stranmillis College. He now lives in Greenisland, Co Antrim with his wife Lynda. He is the author of more than 20 books and booklets on aviation and has written a large number of articles for magazines in the UK, Ireland and the USA. He also reviews books for several publications, gives talks to local history societies, etc and has appeared on TV and radio programmes, discussing aspects of aviation history. His first aviation memory is of a helicopter landing on Islandmagee in about 1958/59. He was much too young to identify it so if any reader can help he would be very pleased to hear from them.

Ernie driving a Ferguson TE20 in 1949.

Ernie Cromie's almost lifelong interest in all things aeronautical was initially inspired by the sight and sound of a Royal Air Force Halifax bomber from the Meteorological Squadron at Aldergrove circling over farm livestock trapped by deep snow drifts around his home, in the foothills of Slieve Croob in Co Down, during the unforgettably bad winter of 1947. Twelve years later, when he was a member of the Army Cadet Force, his first-ever flight was in a RAF Anson aircraft at Jurby, Isle of Man. Unable to realise his boyhood ambition to become a pilot in the RAF because of defective eyesight, he had a fulfilling career as a town planner in the Northern Ireland Civil Service but never lost his enthusiasm for all things aviation. He has been a member of the Ulster Aviation Society since 1979, serving as its Chairman for 30 years until 2012 when he relinquished all executive responsibility in order to devote more time to researching the history of aviation in Northern Ireland, with particular reference to the United States Army Air Force and Naval Air Service presence there during the Second World War. He has written numerous articles for a wide range of aviation journals and other publications, and this is his third book.

The authors would like to extend their particular thanks and sincere appreciation to all the staff at Colourpoint Books, to Paul McMaster for his research in the Bombardier Belfast photograph archive, to Alan McKnight of Bombardier and Ian Montgomery of the Public Record Office, Belfast, for facilitating the use of selected images from the archive and finally to the former Company Secretary of Shorts, Gordon Bruce, for access to his detailed personal records of the Company's activities.

If this book encourages you to take a deeper interest in aviation in Northern Ireland, past and present, you may wish to join the **Ulster Aviation Society**. You can explore the information, history, events and aircraft owned by the society at:

www.ulsteraviationsociety.org

FOREWORD

THE DEVELOPMENT OF manufacturing industry and transport technology are aspects of Irish history which have received comparatively little attention. This is unfortunate, because there are parts of the island, notably in Ulster/Northern Ireland, where, for generations, the manufacture of products for sale and export has been a significant aspect of economic growth and development. Whereas some industries that were formerly pre-eminent have decreased in importance, shipbuilding for instance, others have blossomed or at least remain competitive despite problems resulting from the process of globalisation, not least its implications for continuing investment in local companies.

The aviation and aerospace industry is in the latter category and has its origins in the determined efforts of aviators like AV Roe and Samuel Cody in England and a certain Henry George 'Harry' Ferguson from Co Down, to design, build and successfully fly aircraft during the pioneering years 1908/09 in the United Kingdom. In 1909, the Short Brothers obtained a licence from the American Wright Brothers to build six Wright biplanes in a factory in Kent and by the outbreak of the First World War there were at least 10 aircraft manufacturing firms in Great Britain. In 1916, shipbuilders Harland & Wolff in Belfast were awarded contracts to manufacture aircraft for the Royal Flying Corps and Royal Naval Air Service and 20 years later this was a significant factor which led to the creation of Short & Harland, the result of a merger with Short Brothers.

From such early developments emerged Northern Ireland's aircraft manufacturing and aerospace industry which today is comprised of numerous companies designing and manufacturing a diverse range of products. For the most part, the businesses involved are based exclusively in Northern Ireland, reflecting perhaps the spirit of individual initiative exemplified by the achievements of local men and women such as Harry Ferguson, Lilian Bland, James Martin and Rex McCandless whose achievements are featured in this book. Historically, the aviation industry in Northern Ireland has built a wide range of aircraft, some of which have been unique or ground-breaking, the Shorts SC.1 vertical take-off aircraft, for example. Happily, some of these products have been preserved for posterity, in the Ulster Folk & Transport Museum at Cultra and the Ulster Aviation Collection at Maze/Long Kesh which is now the home of the research aircraft the Short SB.4, only one of which was built, to investigate the properties of a unique form of wing.

The story of how the industry has grown and developed is a fascinating one, outlined in the pages that follow by expanded captions that accompany and interpret more than 320 photographs, a high proportion of which have not been published before. The authors have made good use of the material at their disposal and it is obvious they have researched the topic meticulously, the book being a timely reminder of the widespread nature of the industry and its importance to the local economy. I congratulate them.

James Martin, CBE, FREng, MA, BAI, FRAeS, CEng
Joint Managing Director
Martin-Baker Aircraft Company Limited

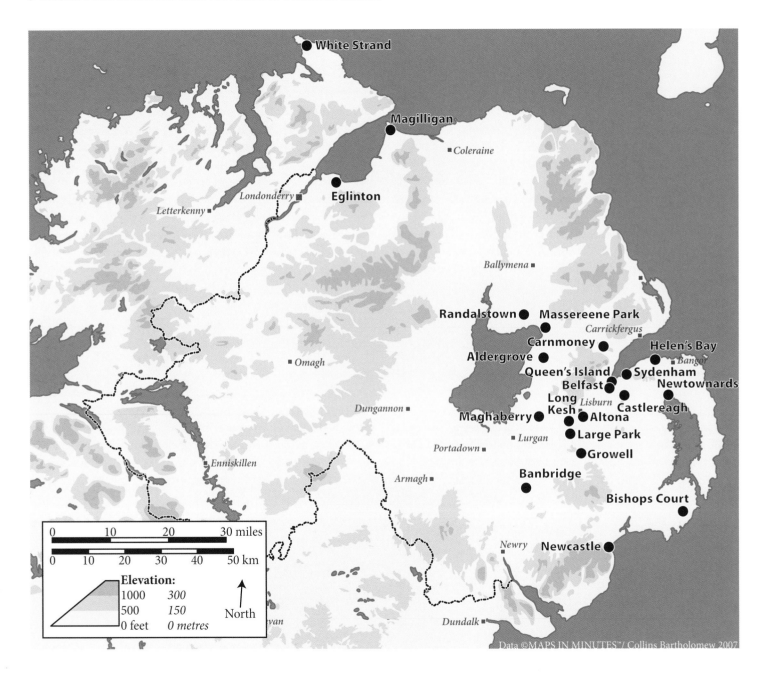

INTRODUCTION

THE FIRST STEPS in the manufacture of heavier-than-air, powered flying machines in Ireland were carried out by three remarkable people in their private workshops, just as the Edwardian era was drawing to a close. There is a view, particularly in the North-West, that the first Irishman to build and fly his own heavier-than-air craft was Joseph Cordner, who was born at Derryinver, Co Armagh in 1875 and who established bicycle shops in Lurgan in 1900 and then in Londonderry in 1908. His exploits on the White Strand between Lisfarnon and Buncrana in Co Donegal have been covered with a veil of obscurity. However, recent research by Michael Clarke has been able to demonstrate that Cordner built and tested three monoplanes of his own design during the period 1908–1912. The monoplanes' wings, which were constructed to an unusual triangular lattice design and incorporated v-shaped ducts, were part of a patented control system. They were powered firstly by a 35 hp JAP (JA Prestwich of London) engine and then by a 50 hp Anzani.

It would appear that his series of experiments terminated following an accident in 1912 at Eglinton, when the Cordner 'Special' broke free from its tethers when the engine was being run up and crashed, pilotless into a tree. No firm date can be established nor is there evidence to show that the flights were any more than short hops of up to 100 yards, though it is contended that two local boys were taken up as passengers on separate occasions.

Therefore, subject to further conclusive evidence being produced, it is generally accepted that on 31 December 1909, Harry Ferguson, who was born in 1884 at Growell, Co Down, made the first successful aeroplane flight in Ireland, in a monoplane of his own design, powered by an eight-cylinder, 35 hp, air-cooled JAP engine at Large Park, Hillsborough, Co Down. The *Belfast Evening Telegraph* reported on 1 January 1910, "The first successful flight of an Irish built and owned aeroplane has been accomplished. It is, in fact, the first flight of an aeroplane in this country." The newspaper described

Joe Cordner at Buncrana. *(M Clarke Collection)*

Harry Ferguson at Hillsborough. *(Guy Warner Collection)*

the actual flight with more enthusiasm than aeronautical understanding,

> "The machine was set against the wind and all force being developed, the splendid pull of the new propeller swept the big aeroplane along as Mr Ferguson advanced the lever. Presently at the movement of the pedal, the aeroplane rose into the air at a height of from nine to twelve feet amidst the hearty cheers of the onlookers. The poise of the machine was perfect and Mr Ferguson made a splendid flight of about 130 yards. Although fierce winds made the machine wobble a little twice, the navigator steadied her by bringing her head into wind. Then he brought the machine down to earth safely after having accomplished probably the most successful initial flight that has ever been attempted upon an aeroplane."

Unfortunately, the undulating and hilly terrain at Hillsborough wasn't particularly suitable for flying so Harry continued his experiments in Massereene Park at Antrim. By April 1910, he had sufficient confidence in his personal and the machine's capability that he gave short flights to a couple of Boy Scouts who were encamped nearby.

Harry Ferguson at Newcastle in July 1910. *(Ernie Cromie Collection)*

But his need of access to more suitable flying locations remained and in early June he commenced flying from Magilligan, which proved to be an almost ideal venue. In July however, he was persuaded by the offer of a prize of £100 to fly his aircraft for a distance of two miles at Newcastle, Co Down. His initial attempts were unsuccessful for, as the *Belfast Evening Telegraph* noted, "Mr Harry Ferguson made two good flights at Newcastle on Saturday though the second of these was rudely terminated when he sustained damage to a wheel and propeller on landing." Undeterred, by 8 August 1910 he was back at Newcastle where, with a repaired and overhauled aircraft, he flew well over two miles along the beach at a height of between 50 and 100 feet and won the prize. This, incidentally, was Ireland's first officially observed flight. Further successful flights were made at Magilligan Strand, Co Londonderry, though he had another scare when he lost height over Lough Foyle and actually touched the water. He kept the throttle wide open and managed to coax the aircraft back into the air. A contemporary newspaper report stated,

> "No sooner was the descent made than Mr Ferguson switched on his engine and splashing along the water, the lower part of the aeroplane submerged and the propeller deluging him with spray, he rose clear of the tide amidst the applause of the spectators and regained the beach."

In October of that year he had a setback at Magilligan with a crash that left his machine a wreck. He flew again in 1911, undertaking to appear at the North Down Agricultural Society Show at Newtownards on 15 June. While practising a few days earlier he had to make a forced landing on the sands. The aeroplane was taken to James Miskelly's farm nearby – close to the site of what would become Ards Airfield. The undercarriage was repaired and a new propeller was fitted. Ferguson resumed flying and took up a passenger on two flights. Sadly he came to grief again with the result that only

A replica of the Ferguson Flyer used to hang from the ceiling at Belfast International Airport. *(Guy Warner Collection)*

the wrecked aeroplane could be displayed at the show as a sorry looking static exhibit.

He returned to Newtownards for the same purpose in October and was more successful but his time as a pioneer aviator was almost at an end. A full-size replica of the Ferguson monoplane was constructed many years later by another renowned Irish airman, Captain Jack Kelly-Rogers. For some years it made a splendid sight, suspended above the concourse of Belfast International Airport at Aldergrove.

Ferguson was matched over the period 1909–11 by the intrepid lady aeronaut, Lilian Bland, who was born in Kent in 1878, but came to live in Carnmoney, Co Antrim and who also designed and flew her own aircraft, the first biplane constructed in Ireland and the first aeroplane to be designed, built and tested by a woman anywhere. She was a remarkable personality who had already made a name for herself in London as a press photographer and sports writer.

Back home in Carnmoney this grand-daughter of the Irish

Gentry further astonished her contemporaries by wearing riding breeches, smoking cigarettes in public, tinkering with motor car engines and riding astride rather than side-saddle. All of these characteristics were sufficient to make her stand out anywhere in the British Isles during the Edwardian period and rather more so in Presbyterian Ulster. She had become interested in aviation through her hobby of photographing bird life; in particular she had become fascinated by the seagulls wheeling in the skies over the Western Isles of Scotland.

During the winter of 1909–10 she designed and manufactured her aeroplane from spruce, ash, elm and bamboo, covered with unbleached calico, which she doped with a home-mixed concoction of gelatine and formalin.

The 'Mayfly' was flown as a glider in the spring of 1910 on the slopes of Carnmoney Hill, with the assistance of her aunt's gardener's boy, Joe Blain, who was her chief helper and, subsequently, four stalwart members of the Royal Irish Constabulary. Their job was to hold on to the glider after the initial series of tethered flights had been successfully accomplished by Lilian Bland and Joe Blain. The lifting qualities of the 'Mayfly' were so good that the four constables were in danger of becoming test pilots, so they released their hold with great alacrity, leaving Joe

Lilian Bland in her overalls. *(Flight Magazine)*

Blain to cling on, turn the glider out of wind and bring it back to earth.

Convinced by the demonstration that she was on the right path, Lilian Bland then wrote to the aviation pioneer AV Roe, asking if he could supply her with a two-stroke, air-cooled engine. In July she caught the ferry to England and returned with a 20 hp engine and propeller. Two other passengers on the boat train asked the purpose of her baggage – "To make an aeroplane." she replied. "What is an aeroplane?" was the response.

The engine was test run with the aid of her aunt's ear trumpet and a whiskey bottle filled with petrol. An engine mounting was added to the trailing edge of the lower wing, a canvas seat was furnished for the leading edge, a T-bar control yoke was fitted and a tricycle undercarriage was constructed. The 'Mayfly' was configured as a pusher with the engine behind the pilot.

The small field at Carnmoney was judged to be inadequate for flight trials, instead Lord O'Neill's 800 acre park at Randalstown was made available. The first tentative hops were made in August 1910. At first the aviatrix could scarcely

Lilian in the 'Mayfly' 1910. *(Ulster Aviation Society)*

believe that she had left the ground until viewing the evidence – as the cessation and resumption of the wheel tracks denoted her flightpath. The flights increased in length to nearly a quarter of a mile and the *Belfast Evening Telegraph* declared on 7 September:

> "First Irish Biplane to Fly. Co Antrim Lady's Successes in Aviation. Since the aeroplane has been on its flying ground the weather has been most unfavourable but the machine at its first trial rose from the ground after a run of thirty feet and flew for some distance a few feet above the ground. The machine is built somewhat on the lines of a Curtiss biplane but has two elevators working separately or together in connection with the horizontal tailplanes."

Lilian Bland certainly aspired to seek commercial opportunities, placing an advert in *Flight* magazine early in 1911.

However, both Lilian Bland and Harry Ferguson turned their back on aviation after these achievements, neither attempted to gain Aviators' Certificates issued by the Royal Aero Club. Nevertheless, Ferguson produced eight variants of his aircraft, including the prototype but of course he became more famous for his invention of the Three-Point Linkage and its role in the development of the modern agricultural tractor, while in 1911 Lilian Bland was bribed by the offer of a motor car from her father to pursue less hazardous activities. Joseph Cordner, on the other hand, elected to undergo pilot training at the Hall School of Flying at Hendon Aerodrome and was awarded his certificate in September 1916. His flying exploits in 1919 are described in Volume II of this history. He died at the age of 88 in 1960. Harry Ferguson was 76 years old when he passed away in 1960, and Lilian Bland died in 1971 at the age of 92. A more detailed account of her adventurous life may be found in *Lilian Bland* by Guy Warner.

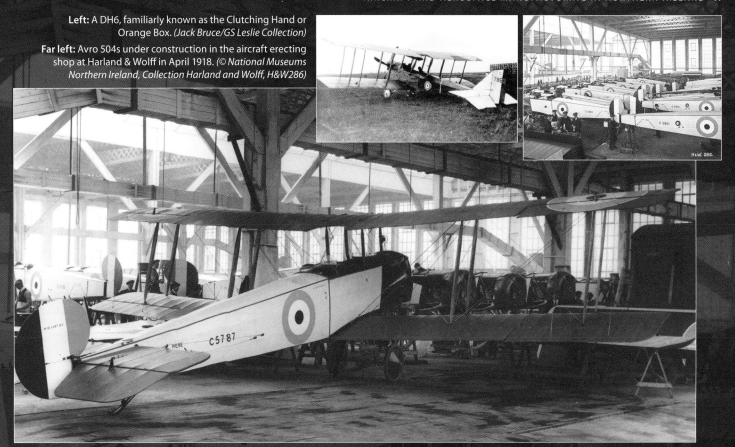

Left: A DH6, familiarly known as the Clutching Hand or Orange Box. *(Jack Bruce/GS Leslie Collection)*

Far left: Avro 504s under construction in the aircraft erecting shop at Harland & Wolff in April 1918. *(© National Museums Northern Ireland, Collection Harland and Wolff, H&W286)*

Avro 504J C5787, one of a batch of 300 constructed at Harland & Wolff. *(© National Museums Northern Ireland, Collection Harland and Wolff, H&W283)*

During the First World War, the value of the aeroplane in combat was ever more widely realised, with the result that demand rapidly increased the output of the existing aircraft companies. It therefore became necessary to outsource production, using established engineering companies to build the designs of others. The first large-scale aircraft manufacturers in Northern Ireland were the world renowned shipbuilders, Harland & Wolff. They commenced in 1917 with the construction of an eventual total of 300 single-engine DH6s (C5451-C5750) and at least 500 Avro 504Js and Ks (C5751-C6050 and E301-E600), which were shipped by sea to England. The old model office was converted into an aeroplane drawing office, the ships' electric store was cleared to become a shop for the erection of fuselages and the joiners' shop was pressed into service. The Works' Joint Committee of the Furniture Trades Union drew up a list of its members in Belfast whose skills could be used in working with wood, fabric and wire. The first complete aircraft manufactured and assembled by the company was a DH6, finished on 9 October 1917. The Avro 504 is justly famous as one of the classic aircraft of its era, which lasted from before the Great War until the 1930s; the DH6 is much less heralded but gave useful service as a trainer and on coastal anti-submarine patrol duties.

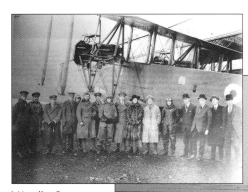

Belfast docks viewed from the roof of the Midland Hotel on York Road in 1917. *(GR Volkert)*

A Handley Page V/1500 at Aldergrove. *(© National Museums Northern Ireland, Collection Harland and Wolff, H&W464)*

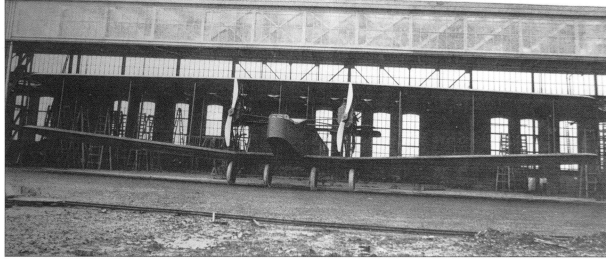

A V/1500 at Aldergrove outside the aircraft shed. *(© National Museums Northern Ireland, Collection Harland and Wolff, H&W456)*

By 1917, Handley Page O/100 and O/400 twin-engine heavy bombers were being produced in quantity for the RFC and RNAS. In August of that year, the War Cabinet authorised the construction of three prototypes of an even larger machine. As the Handley Page (HP) factory in Cricklewood in North London was working to full capacity, it was decided to make use of the expert draughtsmen, carpenters and fitters of Harland & Wolff. To this end, the Chief Designer, GR Volkert, travelled to Belfast to take charge of the project at the head of a team from HP, while Frederick Handley Page himself visited the city every weekend to monitor progress. In February 1918, Aldergrove (170 acres of farmland, 16 miles west of Belfast, close to Lough Neagh and the village of Crumlin which had been purchased

for development as an airfield for the Royal Flying Corps in 1917) was selected as the site for the flying test field, with the result that the construction of final assembly hangars was needed. The flight sheds were not ready in time for the first prototype – though when completed, Aldergrove had one of the largest hangars in the British Isles, measuring over 500 feet long. The first massive HP V/1500, B9463, was transported in parts to Cricklewood (the fuselage was shipped directly to London but the wings went by way of the steamer, the *Princess Maud*, from Larne and then by rail to Euston) where it flew for the first time on 22 May 1918. Five further aircraft were sent by sea to be assembled and flown in London.

This Harland & Wolff built V/1500, seen here at RAF Bircham Newton in 1919, made a round-Britain endurance flight piloted by Capt HC Vereker. *(Guy Warner Collection)*

The first V/1500 to fly from Aldergrove (now No 16 Aircraft Acceptance Park) was E4304, which took to the air on 20 December 1918, powered by its four 375 hp Rolls-Royce Eagle engines. It was in the experienced hands of Clifford Prodger, HP's 28-year-old American test pilot, "on a circular tour, passing over Divis Mountain. At two o'clock the aeroplane was right over the city and was an object of intense curiosity, the observers including thousands of mill hands and office workers." The aircraft was entirely satisfactory and departed for RAF Bircham Newton in Norfolk the next day (the base of No 166 and 167 Squadrons), to be followed by E4308 on 18 January 1919 with a crew of 7½ tons of freight on board. The V/1500 was a masterpiece of contemporary technology, weighing 13½ tons. It had a wingspan of 126 feet and a fuselage length of 64 feet, it carried a crew of six and was capable of lifting 7500 lbs of bombs 1300 miles. It had an endurance of 17 hours in the air and had a top speed of 99 mph. Its four undercarriage wheels were each five feet in diameter. The last fully documented Harland & Wolff built V/1500 was J6573, which was powered by Napier Lions and was flown from Aldergrove by Major Keith Park on 3 September 1919. However, it appears that two further V/1500s, piloted by Park again and Wing Commander Sholto Douglas departed from Aldergrove in June 1920. The best estimate is that eight V/1500s were flown from Aldergrove and five were shipped to Cricklewood, from an original contract for 20 aircraft, plus the components for a complete O/400, J1934.

Oswald Short. *(Bombardier Belfast)*

Sir Frederick Rebbeck (left) with the First Lord of the Admiralty, AV Alexander. *(Bombardier Belfast)*

The Short & Harland factory under construction in 1937. *(Bombardier Belfast)*

It would be almost 20 years before aircraft manufacturing would return. A Defence White Paper, published in March 1935, recommended the dispersal of aircraft factories as far to the north-west of London as possible. The construction of these was to be paid for by the government. It was quite rightly believed that as the major threat to the UK would come from the east, the productive capacity of the country had to be protected from bombing and distributed more widely. Moreover, it was recognised that the Royal Air Force was in need of more modern equipment in much greater quantities. Short Brothers of Rochester were already seriously considering a move to South Wales. Frederick Rebbeck, the

Chairman of Harland & Wolff, which at that time was the largest shipyard in the world, was also very keen to discuss the possibility of starting an aircraft factory in the Belfast area. The Northern Ireland Government encouraged the company to enter into discussions with the Air Ministry. Colonel HAP Disney, an official from the Ministry visited Queen's Island and made a favourable report on the facilities. It was believed that a combination with aircraft manufacturers Short Brothers of Rochester would match knowledge and facilities for the production and building of flying boats. Moreover, in November 1935, the decision had been made to commence work on a new aerodrome adjacent to the shipyard at Sydenham on claimed land

Sir Kingsley Wood arrives at Sydenham. *(Belfast Harbour* Commissioners)

The Short Scion Senior G-AECU. *(Bombardier Belfast)*

John Lankester Parker. *(Bombardier Belfast)*

on the southern shore of Belfast Lough. The plan to establish a factory at Milford Haven was abandoned and on 2 June 1936 Short & Harland Limited was incorporated under the Northern Ireland Companies Act, owned 60% by Shorts and 40% by Harland & Wolff. On 29 July 1936 Oswald Short, the Managing Director and sole survivor of the three brothers, was flown by the company Chief Test Pilot, John Lankester Parker, from Rochester to Newtownards in a Short S.22 Scion Senior, G-AECU. The first piles for the new factory were driven the following month, with the commencement of the erection of steelwork in October. The initial construction was not publicly funded though the subsequent enlargement of the factory in 1938–1941 was. By August 1937, the first aircraft components were being produced. The workforce numbered 1392 by the end of the year. On 11 September 1937, Notice to Airmen No 197 was issued by the Air Ministry, which confirmed the issue of a public-use licence for the airfield. On 15 August 1938 the Minister for Air, Sir Kingsley Wood, visited Sydenham to inspect progress, by which time more than 5000 workers were employed. Until 1947 all of the Belfast company's aircraft work would, on Air Ministry directive, be subcontracted from Short Brothers (Rochester & Bedford) Ltd.

Bombays under construction in the Belfast factory's 120 foot bay. (Bombardier Belfast)

An engine test for Bombay L5808. (Bombardier Belfast)

The interior of a Bombay. (Bristol Aeroplane Company via Bombardier Belfast)

Short & Harland began large-scale production of military aircraft with licence-built Bristol Type 130 Bombays. Work commenced in Belfast in the second half of 1937. In November 1938, it was believed that the aircraft would have to be dismantled and taken by road to Aldergrove to be test-flown from the macadam runways there but, in the event, the first flight of L5808 was on 3 March 1939, at Sydenham. This was one of a contract for 50 of this type, reduced from an original requirement for 80. Designed by the Bristol Company as a bomber-transport, it was thus the first aircraft to be built at the new factory and to fly from there. Major components were also manufactured by Harland & Wolff. All were delivered between April 1939 and June 1940 at a price of £24,136 each. It was a twin-engine, high-wing monoplane with a fixed undercarriage and was powered by a pair of 1010 hp Pegasus engines. In the trooping role, 24 soldiers could be carried, alternatively the seats could be removed and 10 stretchers accommodated as an air ambulance. A rail was fitted along the cabin roof from which aeroengines could be slung in a specialised cargo carrying fit. Provision was also made to install water or fuel tanks. More aggressively, up to 2000 lbs of bombs could be loaded on racks fitted underneath the fuselage. Bombays saw active service in the Libyan campaign of 1940 and also assisted in the evacuation of the Greek royal family from Crete to Egypt. In addition to their transport duties, the Bombays also carried out night-bombing sorties all along the North African coast and in Eritrea. They flew supplies to the beleaguered island of Malta, troops into Habbaniya to reinforce the garrison that was under siege from Raschid Ali's Iraqi forces and in November 1941 made the first airborne para-drop in the Middle East at Timini. Supplies were also flown deep behind enemy lines in 1942 to support advanced units. An unsung and rather forgotten type, the Bombays gave good service with Nos 117, 216 and 271 Squadrons of the Royal Air Force and also with No 1 Australian Air Ambulance Unit (evacuating over 2000 casualties from North Africa and Sicily and later carrying nursing sisters to Italy after the Anzio landings) until being struck off charge in August 1944.

The Hampden second prototype, L7271, having had new engines fitted, flies past the civil hangar at Sydenham on 20 February 1939. *(Bombardier Belfast)*

Four Herefords and a Bombay at Sydenham. *(Bombardier Belfast, courtesy of the Belfast Telegraph)*

The next new aircraft to emerge from Sydenham was on 19 May 1939, when the Handley Page Hereford, L6002, took to the sky, flown by the Shorts' test pilot Harold 'Pip' Piper, the first of 150 of these twin-engine medium bombers to be built in Belfast, with sub-contract work also being given to Harland & Wolff, Combe Barbour and James Mackie & Sons. In the case of the shipyard, this was carried out in the Alexandra Works, where the V/1500s had been built some 20 years before. On 16 July 1937, the second prototype Hampden, L7271, had been flown into Sydenham to be modified by Short & Harland as the prototype Hereford; Pip Piper being at the controls for its first flight on 6 October 1938. Materials for the main production contract were first ordered in May 1937, with production commencing a couple of months later. All the Herefords were delivered between August 1939 and September 1940.

Due principally to problems associated with its unconventional and unreliable, air-cooled, in-line, 1000 hp Napier Dagger engines, the Hereford did not have a very active career, serving only a few months with No 185 Squadron before being restricted to crew training duties with No 16 Operational Training Unit at Upper Heyford. Like the Avro Manchester, it was basically a good airframe with a bad engine. The main Hampden variant with Bristol Pegasus engines was much more successful as a medium bomber. The tail boom of L6012 was subsequently attached to the Hampden P1344, which is undergoing restoration at the RAF Museum, Cosford and is therefore the earliest surviving aerostructure built by Short & Harland. Air Ministry plans to build the de Havilland DH95 Hertfordshire and the Armstrong Whitworth AW41 Albemarle in Belfast did not come to fruition.

WP Kemp, the General Manager (left), presenting W Browning, the Works Manager to HRH The Duke of Kent (wearing hat). Company Secretary, EWA Woolmer is next in line. *(Bombardier Belfast)*

A section of the large crowd at the exhibition park in July 1939. *(Bombardier Belfast)*

The *Aeroplane* magazine reported on 'A Celebration In Belfast' held from 28–29 July 1939. As well as viewing a flying display programme at Sydenham, Captain Harold Balfour, the Under Secretary of State for Air, was taken on a tour of Shorts' factory with other dignitaries, including the Prime Minister of Northern Ireland, Lord Craigavon, hosted by Oswald Short and Frederick Rebbeck. The *Aeroplane's* correspondent was much impressed by all that he witnessed, from the size of the factory to the aerobatics performed by Sergeant Ken Mackenzie in a Hawker Hind and the 'spectacular flypast' by Pip Piper in a Hereford. Balfour was deputising for his Secretary of State, Sir Kingsley Wood, who had suffered an unfortunate accident when flying over to Belfast. His DH86, L7596, of No 24 Squadron had crash-landed on a hillside in Cumberland. His fellow passengers included Air Marshal Sir Christopher Courtney and Air Vice Marshal

Sholto Douglas. Courtney's injury prevented him succeeding Air Chief Marshal Dowding as C-in-C Fighter Command. Dowding thereby remained in post during the Battle of Britain. A rather more prosaic assessment was given by EWA Woolmer, the Company Secretary in Belfast: "Many were the difficulties in those early days, which would have daunted less hardy spirits. We sometimes recall with mixed feelings the approach to the temporary offices. This was something of an adventure, especially in wet weather, as a false step from the plank gangway meant an ankle deep paddle in thick mud. In addition, despite Belfast's undoubted reputation for freedom from snow, this particular year the city experienced the worst snowfall for years. The enthusiasm of the workers, clad in overcoats etc allowed work to proceed but no enthusiasm could overcome the impossible task of working ankle deep in snow."

A CRO salvage dinghy in the Musgrave Channel. *(Bombardier Belfast)*

The first aircraft to use the slipway in Belfast on 12 November 1940 was this Supermarine Walrus destined for the CRO. *(Bombardier Belfast)*

Employees from the Lambeg facility take a closer look at a Spitfire. *(Bombardier Belfast)*

Another activity at Sydenham which would assume major importance began during this period, the Civilian Repair Organisation (CRO), which between 1940 and 1947 received 784 aircraft of 55 different types for repair or scrapping after accidents or battle damage. They came in all shapes and sizes including Avro Ansons, Bristol Blenheims, Consolidated Catalinas, Fairey Battles, Gloster Gladiators, Grumman Hellcats, Hawker Hurricanes, Miles Martinets, Short Stirlings, Short Sunderlands, Supermarine Spitfires, Supermarine Walrus, Vickers Wellingtons and Westland Lysanders. At various times outstations functioned at Aldergrove, Ballyhalbert, Ballykelly, Bishops Court, Castle Archdale, Limavady, Maghaberry, Mallusk and St Angelo. The CRO was formed, within the UK as a whole, under the leadership of Lord Nuffield, to repair damaged aircraft, return them to active service and so maximise the number available for front-line duties. By this means, some of the pressure on the aircraft manufacturing industry was relieved. During the war, it has been estimated that the CROs nation-wide repaired over 80,000 aircraft.

The first Stirling, N6000, is rolled out of the 120 ft bay on 9 October 1940. *(Bombardier Belfast)*

CPT Lipscomb, who was employed at Rochester and then Belfast from 1914 to 1951, rising to the position of Technical Director. *(Bombardier Belfast)*

Stirling N6000 crossing the bridge to the Flight & Service Hangar on 9 October 1940. *(Bombardier Belfast)*

The workforce at Shorts increased in size considerably to 5735 in 1938 and 8451 in 1939, and began to gear up for tasks of much more importance than the Bombay and Hereford – the Short S.29 Stirling heavy bomber and the Short S.25 Sunderland flying boat. The first of the two most significant types to be manufactured in Belfast during the war was the Short Stirling, for which the initial contract was placed on 4 May 1938. The first Stirling to be built at Sydenham was N6000, which flew for the first time on 18 October 1940. On the night of 10/11 February 1941, the Stirling became the first four-engine monoplane heavy bomber to enter operational service with the RAF

when three aircraft of No 7 Squadron attacked oil storage tanks at Rotterdam. It was a highly manoeuvrable aircraft for its size but due to Air Ministry insistence at the design stage, against the advice of the designer, CPT Lipscomb, that the wingspan should not exceed 100 feet, rather than the proposed 112 feet – so that it would fit into existing hangars – it had a less than desirable maximum ceiling. It was powered by four 1650 hp Bristol Hercules engines and could carry a maximum bomb load of 14,000 lbs. The Stirling was, however, well loved by its crews, particularly because of its ability to sustain heavy battle damage and still make it home. Two posthumous Victoria

Stirlings under construction in the 160 ft bay in January 1941. *(Bombardier Belfast)*

Ladies from one of the fabrication plants in Lisburn
in front of a Stirling on a visit to the main factory.
(Bombardier Belfast)

Crosses were won by Stirling pilots, Flight Sergeant RH Middleton Royal Australian Air Force of No 149 Squadron flying BF372 and Flight Sergeant AL Aaron in EF452 of No 218 Squadron. The aircraft was particularly suitable for mine-laying duties; primarily in Danish waters, where channels linked the Baltic and North Seas. The last bombing raid involving Stirlings was in 1944, thereafter it gave valuable service as an electronic countermeasures platform, clandestine operations dropping personnel or supplies, and as a paratroop transport and glider tug, taking a full part in the airborne assaults on D-Day, over Arnhem and the Rhine Crossing. The men of the Glider Pilot Regiment had a great deal of respect for the Stirling Mk IV, which also was used in 1945 to bring home liberated POWs and demobilising servicemen. Its final role was as a transport, with the last Mk V being phased out of RAF service in July 1946. The last Stirling to be built was a Mk V, PK186, which took to the air on 8 December 1945. Remarkably the Stirling went to war again in 1948. A dozen Mk Vs had been sold to the Belgian airline Trans-Air in 1947 and six were sold on to the Royal Egyptian Air Force, some of which took part in bombing missions against Israel. In all probability they were scrapped in Cairo in 1951.

Civilian employees of Short & Harland pose beside a Sunderland on 14 June 1943. (*Bombardier Belfast*)

Civilian personnel at work in the cavernous interior of a Sunderland in Belfast. (*Bombardier Belfast*)

Sunderland W6050 emerges from the 300 ft extension on 9 April 1942. (Bombardier Belfast)

The initial batch of Short Sunderland flying boats to be built in Belfast was numbered W6050–W6064, the contract being placed on 28 March 1940 and the first flight taking place from Belfast Lough on 24 April 1942. The prototype, K4774, had flown from the River Medway on 16 October 1937 and was a military development of the renowned C class Empire flying boat. A total of 749 Sunderlands were produced for service with the RAF, Commonwealth and Allied air forces. They flew many thousands of convoy escort and anti-submarine patrols over the North Sea, the Atlantic, the Mediterranean and the Indian Ocean from the first day of the war to the last. The initial U-boat kill from the air was U-55 by a Sunderland of No 228 Squadron on 30 January 1940, the first of a total of 46 sinkings achieved by the type, some of which were, of course, shared with naval vessels. The last was U-242 on 30 April 1945. Without the Sunderland, it may be contended, the Battle of the Atlantic might never have been won. Some measure of the Sunderland's fighting qualities may be gained from an epic air battle over the Bay of Biscay on 2 June 1943, when the crew of Mk III, EJ134, of No 461 Squadron RAAF fought off attacks from eight formidable German Ju88s, shooting down three and damaging three more. The remaining two broke off the attack,

Sunderlands under construction in November 1944. *(Bombardier Belfast)*

The fuselage of a Sunderland being transported through Belfast. *(Bombardier Belfast)*

leaving the Sunderland the victor, though badly damaged itself. The German nickname for the Sunderland was the 'Flying Porcupine'. A total of 132 Sunderlands were built at Sydenham, consisting of: Mk II (15), Mk III (69) and Mk V (48). The Mk IIs and IIIs were powered by 1065 hp Bristol Pegasus engines, while the Mk Vs were fitted with 1200 hp Pratt and Whitney Twin Wasp engines. The final Sunderland, SZ599, was launched at Queen's Island on 14 June 1946. They served in the RAF until 1959 – in the Berlin Airlift, the Yangtse Incident in 1949, the Korean War, with the British North Greenland Expedition and in the Far East. They returned regularly to Shorts for modification and to Lough Erne for training. Queen's Island said a final good-bye to the Sunderland on 21 December 1957, when an example belonging to the French Naval Air Service, Aéronavale, was serviced for the last time. Sunderlands continued to serve with Aéronavale until 1960 and the Royal New Zealand Air Force until 1967. ML824, which was launched at Queen's Island in June 1944 and served with No 201 Squadron at Castle Archdale, No 330 Squadron in Norway and Aéronavale in West Africa, is preserved in the Royal Air Force Museum, Hendon.

The 160 ft bay after the Luftwaffe blitz. *(Bombardier Belfast)*

Further bombing damage in 1941. *(Bombardier Belfast)*

The harbour area had been the focus of considerable German reconnaissance activity and was subjected to three serious bombing raids in April/May 1941. A total of 35 bomb craters temporarily put RAF Sydenham out of action. A single parachute oil bomb hit the aeroplane fuselage factory and destroyed the four and a half acre shed, the main assembly jigs, machine tools and parts for the fuselages of about 50 Stirlings. Five nearly complete Stirlings were so badly damaged that they were deleted from the contract and replacements ordered. By this time the workforce had swelled to more than 11,000. After the Belfast Blitz, 11 dispersed sites were established in Co Antrim and Co Down to reduce the likelihood of further air raids disrupting production. In total, 931 Stirlings were

Stirling fuselages at Altona, Lisburn.
(Bombardier Belfast)

Negotiating the road between Altona and Maghaberry posed problems for this Stirling in October 1943. *(Bombardier Belfast)*

Chief Test Pilots Geoffrey Tyson and Harold 'Pip' Piper. *(Bombardier Belfast)*

assembled at Belfast (1940–45), 148 at Maghaberry (1942–45), 134 at Aldergrove (1941–45) and 5 at Long Kesh (1942-43), making a grand total of 1218, which included all of the Mk IVs (for towing gliders and dropping parachutists) and Vs (transports). Most of the Stirlings and Sunderlands were test flown in Belfast by Geoffrey Tyson and the New Zealander, Pip Piper. Piper alone was responsible for over 800 Stirlings and about 100 Sunderlands, while Tyson furthered his knowledge of the Stirling's operational performance by flying on a bombing raid on Cassel in a Stirling flown by Wing Commander 'Bobbie' Gilmour DSO, DFC, who flew the type with Nos 7, 15 and 218 Squadrons. Tyson succeeded John Lankester Parker as Chief Test Pilot in 1945.

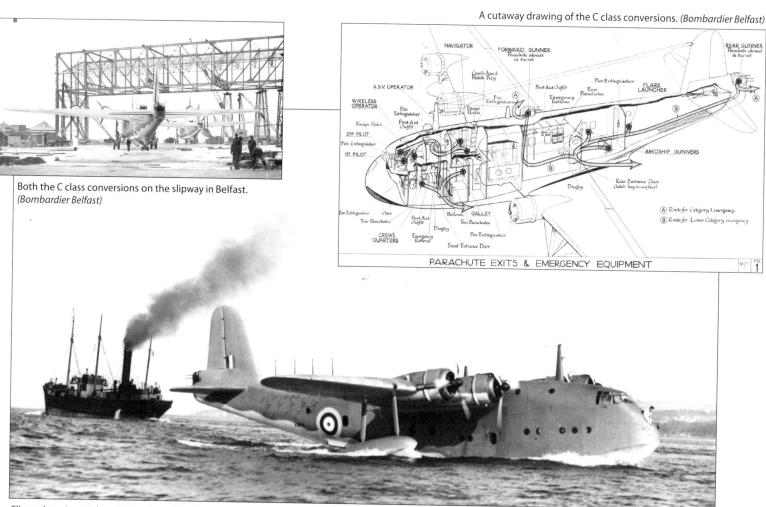

Both the C class conversions on the slipway in Belfast. *(Bombardier Belfast)*

A cutaway drawing of the C class conversions. *(Bombardier Belfast)*

PARACHUTE EXITS & EMERGENCY EQUIPMENT

Clio undergoing trials on Belfast Lough in March 1941. *(Bombardier Belfast)*

Two of Shorts' magnificent S.23 Empire class flying boats were converted for war work at Belfast in 1940–41. Apparently Belfast Harbour Commissioners were most upset when the first of the pair alighted in Belfast Lough on 30 August 1940, not having been given prior notice. A month later *Cordelia* arrived half an hour before receipt of the official notification by Shorts. There was, after all, a war on. G-AETY/AX659, *Clio* and G-AEUD/AX660, *Cordelia*, were equipped with four dorsal radar masts, tail and dorsal gun turrets, redesignated S.23M and pressed into service with No 119 Squadron, patrolling between Bowmore on the Isle of Islay and Iceland. AX659 crashed in Scotland after an engine failure on 22 August 1941. AX660 was used in depth charge trials with 119 Squadron and also served with 413 (RCAF) Squadron. She survived the war and was broken up at Hythe in March 1947.

No 8 Ferry Pool at Sydenham. Photo provided by Stan Watson, one of three ATC cadets whose responsibilities were to keep the following up to date: the weather conditions at all ATA airfields, a card index of airfield serviceability and all safety equipment. Starting rear rank (l-r):

A young Tom Brooke-Smith beside a Gloster Gladiator, which was receiving the attention of the CRO. (*Bombardier Belfast*)

1. Ian Stewart, operations officer, solicitor, and very nice chap.
2. Norman Kelly our MT Driver, who lived off the Ormeau Road. His father ran a dance hall and band. Norman was a tough character, who once threw six rowdies out of the dance hall single-handed.
3. Ron Roberts, a Flight Engineer, who along with John Winston and the ATC cadets, were in Flight Captain Chambers' crew on Sunderlands and Catalinas.
4. Not known
5. John Winston, Flight Engineer. He joined BOAC after the war flying Liberators, Constellations, Stratocruisers, DC7Cs, 707s and 747s. He totalled 20,580 flying hours and was included in the Guinness Book of Records for 1980/3 for having flown the highest number of North Atlantic flights between 1947 and 1978 – 1293 crossings.
6. Eddie Maguire, a pre-war middleweight boxing champion from South Africa.
7. F/O Christopher Lonergan from Eire.
8. Not known
9. Gwynn Jones, a pre-war delay drop parachute champion.
10. Not known
11. John Gilbert
12. Not known
13. Henry Schofield
14. Michael Culhane
16. Not known
17. Not known
18. Biffy Newman, deputy CO
19. Oliver Eric (Paddy) Armstrong, CO
20. Jim McCallum, from South Africa.
21. Satyendra Kumar Roy, from India.
22. Mrs Farquhar, MT driver
23. Bob McKnight, a Sea Cadet from Belfast.
24. Hal Ewing, another Sea Cadet.
25. Eddie Wright, a third Sea Cadet, who joined the Fleet Air Arm and was killed flying in the Mediterranean.

(via Stan Watson)

A significant event in August 1941 was the establishment of No 8 Ferry Pool of the Air Transport Auxiliary (ATA). The Commanding Officer was OE Armstrong, a very well known pre-war airline pilot, indeed it was he who operated the very first Aer Lingus service from Baldonnel to Bristol in the DH84, EI-ABI, *Iolar*, on 27 May 1936. The prime reason for No 8 Pool's existence was the delivery of Short Stirlings from the manufacturer to the RAF but many other types were flown including Vickers Wellington bombers to and from Aldergrove and single-engine fighters from the mainland for loading onto aircraft carriers. The Ferry Pool brought the first contact between a young airman and Sydenham, a location with which he was to become very familiar over the next 20 years, the future Shorts' Chief Test Pilot, Tom Brooke-Smith.

A greetings card showing the Short Empire flying boat, Canopus, over Rochester 1936 by Kenneth Denton, and Oswald Shorts' signature on the card. *(Guy Warner Collection)*

General Manager, WP Kemp (left), with Sir Stafford Cripps (right) outside the Extension Factory in June 1943. *(Bombardier Belfast)*

The number of Shorts' employees in Belfast peaked at 20,750 in January 1943. In the same month a series of important events took place which had great bearing on the way Short Brothers of Rochester and Short & Harland of Belfast were controlled. Sir Strafford Cripps, the Minister of Aircraft Production, firstly ensured that Oswald Short should step down as Chairman of the companies. Government appointees were brought onto the Board of Directors and then all company shares were expropriated, "a swift and utterly ruthless Government take-over that deeply upset Oswald and the other directors and severely shook the morale of the

work-force." Oswald was removed from the board in April 1943 and appointed Honorary Life President, a position which he retained until his death on 4 December 1969 at the age of 86. It is a shameful fact, however, that Oswald was not awarded a knighthood for his services to aviation. Between 1944 and 1946 several government studies and reports were made on the future prospects for Shorts, eventually after considerable prevarication and numerous changes of mind, it was decided in May 1946 that the entire business would transfer from Rochester to Belfast.

Sir Stafford Cripps (second left) and Sir Basil Brooke (second right) visit Nicholson & Bass and inspect a completed drop tank. *(Nicholson & Bass)*

Stirling fin construction at Liddells. *(William Liddell & Co Ltd)*

One of the *Belfast Telegraph* Spitfires. *(Ulster Aviation Society)*

A P-47 with a paper drop tank fitted. *(Ernie Cromie Collection)*

Less well-known than the contribution made by Shorts, a number of other manufacturers in Northern Ireland turned their hand to the production of aviation-related items during the Second World War. The printing company, Nicholson & Bass Ltd, built jettisonable fuel tanks for aircraft, receiving letters of congratulation from Sir Stafford Cripps, the Minister of Aircraft Production and also from Sir Basil Brooke, the Prime Minister of Northern Ireland. The Company later noted that, "We were the only manufacturers of paper fuel tanks in Ireland, and ultimately one of the largest producers in the British Isles. Our production target was 90 tanks per day, or one completed tank every six minutes. All our tanks were made for the United States Army Air Force and in particular, Republic

P-47 Thunderbolts." William Ross & Co, Flax Spinners, not only spun parachute cord but also made components for Short Stirlings, including bomb doors. Stirling parts were also made by the famous Belfast engineering firm, James Mackie & Sons and William Liddell & Co Ltd of Donaghcloney. Other linen firms produced parachute webbing and harnesses, as well as two million flax-fabric parachutes. Harland & Wolff, built not only merchant vessels, warships and aircraft carriers but also over 13 million aircraft parts. The *Belfast Telegraph* Spitfire Fund raised money by public donation between 1940 and 1945 – the eventual total of £88,633 being sufficient to buy 17 aircraft. In commemoration of this, the Ulster Aviation Society, in late 2013, added a full-scale replica of a Spitfire Mk II to its collection.

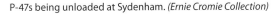

P-38s as deck cargo in the Herdman Channel, Belfast. *(Ernie Cromie Collection)*

P-47s being unloaded at Sydenham. *(Ernie Cromie Collection)*

P-38 Droop Snoot production line at Langford Lodge. *(Ernie Cromie Collection)*

By February, 1939, the Lockheed Aircraft Corporation of California had established a facility at Speke airfield, near Liverpool, to re-assemble and test-fly American aircraft for wartime service with the RAF. Initially, the main aircraft types were twin-engined Lockheed Hudsons and Douglas Bostons, shipped from the USA, disassembled as deck cargo. In the event, because of awkward road connections between Liverpool docks and Speke, it was agreed in November 1940 that assembly of Bostons would be carried out adjacent to Belfast docks, using hangar space at Sydenham. Less than 100 had been assembled and test flown at Sydenham before the assembly facility was closed towards the end of 1941 when Lockheed established a further assembly plant in Scotland. Within a year, however, Lockheed personnel were once again at Sydenham, as a vital component of the air depot which had been established by the company at Langford Lodge in the summer of 1942 to assemble, modify, service and repair a wide variety of American aircraft types that were used operationally by the RAF and USAAF in the UK, mainland Europe and North Africa. Lockheed's role at Belfast docks was to unload P-47 Thunderbolt and P-51 Mustang fighters brought by ship from the USA, assemble them at Sydenham and then fly the

aircraft to Langford Lodge to be modified for operational use. P-38 Lightnings, unloaded on the opposite side of the port at Herdman Channel, were taken to Langford Lodge by road for final assembly. About 1050 American fighter aircraft were imported to and unloaded at Belfast Harbour during the war. Langford Lodge was one of four primary air depots in the UK which handled thousands of aircraft, the broad nature of work on which was described in the first part of this trilogy series of books. However, Langford Lodge was unique in also having a production line where P-38J fighters were converted into the rare, two-seat 'Droop Snoots' during the spring and summer of 1944. This particular variant of the Lightning had the standard nose gun armament removed to make room for a Norden bomb sight and seat for a bomb aimer which enabled one two-seat Droop Snoot to act as a 'master bomber' for a formation of numerous bomb-armed standard P-38Js that would simultaneously drop their bombs when the Droop Snoot was seen to drop its load. In practice, the concept worked well and 26 Droop Snoots were produced at Langford Lodge, plus 100 kits to enable conversions to be carried out elsewhere. Some conversions were carried out as far afield as the India/Burma theatre.

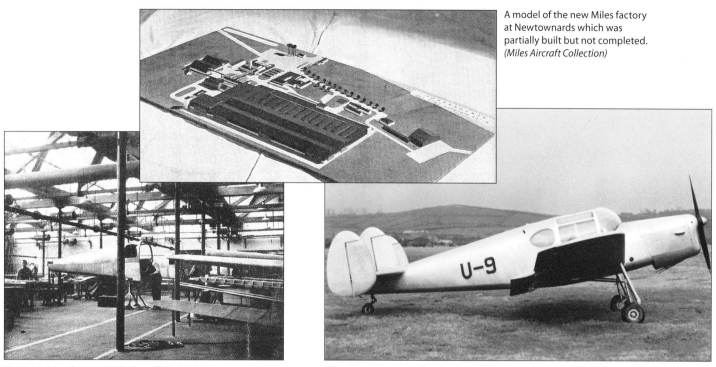

A model of the new Miles factory at Newtownards which was partially built but not completed. *(Miles Aircraft Collection)*

The Banbridge factory. *(Miles Aircraft Collection)*

Miles Messenger at Ards prior to registration. *(Miles Aircraft Collection)*

A new company entered the scene mid-war. Components for the Miles Aircraft Company were made in Banbridge, in a former linen mill, from the autumn of 1943. The first items to be manufactured there were Monoplane Air Tails for air-launched torpedoes. Production of the M.38 Messenger light communications aircraft was commenced in October 1944. The aircraft were assembled and the engines installed at Long Kesh from where the initial test flights of the first five produced were made, the first, RH420, taking to the air in August 1945. They were then ferried to the main Miles airfield at Woodley in England for completion and painting. The first of these was delivered to the RAF in November 1945. Ten Messenger Mk 1s for the RAF were built at Banbridge, as well as a single civil version, G-AHGE, which was built for the Prince Regent of Iraq and fitted out with green leather upholstery. The work was transferred from Banbridge to a new factory by the airfield at Newtownards in

February 1946, from where the test flights of the last five Messengers for the RAF were made. The test pilots in the early days were Ulstermen Wing Commander Terry McComb, OBE and Squadron Leader Eric Esler, DFC. Sixty-five production Messenger Mk 2As, three Mk 4s and a single Mk 4A were built at Newtownards and then flown to Woodley unpainted for final doping and sale. Sadly the operation was closed down in early 1948, following a financial crisis affecting the parent company which forced it into Receivership. The last Ards-built Messenger was ferried to Woodley at the end of May 1948. All that remains at the airfield now is a tail-boom from a Miles M.57 Aerovan, probably G-AJTD, which was blown over in a gale on take-off while transporting a cow to Scotland on 3 November 1948. It is part of the structure supporting the windsock. Two Miles aircraft, the Messenger, G-AJOC and the M.65 Gemini, G-AKEL, are in storage at the Ulster Folk and Transport Museum.

An aerial view of Shorts' Queen's Island facilities. Ranged along the left hand side of Airport Road are the Technical Building, housing engineering departments and drawing offices, the Air Ministry extension factory, the main offices and the main factory. Visible on the airport site are the Flight Shed and Airport Factory (Comet Hangar). The large factory building to the left is part of Harland and Wolff's and served the cranes and slipways of the East Yard, immediately behind it (all of which area now forms Shorts' staff car park). *(Bombardier Belfast)*

A general view of the Design Office in Belfast. *(Bombardier Belfast)*

Shorts became wholly based in Belfast under the name of Short Brothers & Harland Ltd in November 1947, by which time the workforce had more than halved from its level of 11,689 in June 1945. The transfer of the entire operation from Rochester was a huge undertaking, shipping some 3700 tons of material and involving a considerable expansion of the facilities on the Belfast site. The Managing Director later reported to his Board, "Moving factories the size of ours is not a pastime which I would personally recommend." The Main Office, Main Design Office and Main Factory were on Queen's Island, which was connected by a bridge over the water to the Sydenham site, where the airfield, Flight Shed, Engineering & Flight Test Department and Airport Extension Factory were located. The last members of the Rochester Design Office moved to Belfast in summer 1948. Shorts continued to design and construct a

Avro Lincoln SX986 of No 50 Squadron. *(A Thomas Collection)*

The *Golden Hind*, G-AFCI. *(Bombardier Belfast)*

The Main Building. *(Bombardier Belfast)*

wide range of aircraft, some commercially successful, some highly innovative. Early post-war activity included the production of civil airline transport flying boats by converting Sunderlands and Seafords to Sandringhams and Solents. In 1945–46 a major refit was undertaken of G-AFCI, *Golden Hind*, the sole surviving S.26 G class flying boat, preparatory to her re-introduction into service with BOAC. Modification work was also carried out on 90 Avro Lancaster (1945–46) and 49 Avro Lincoln (1946–48) heavy bombers to bring them to the required standard for service in the Far East. In 1944 a contract to build Lincolns (Lancaster Mk IV) in Belfast had been made but was cancelled before any work began.

A cutaway drawing of a Sandringham 1. *(Bombardier Belfast)*

The well-appointed interior of a Sandringham Mk 4's Cabin A looking aft, probably ZK-AMB *Tasman. (Bombardier Belfast via Colin McCarthy)*

BOAC Sandringham 'Portland' on Belfast Lough in April 1947. *(Bombardier Belfast)*

Seventeen S.25 Sunderland Mk III (known as the Hythe class) and 26 Sandringham Mk 1, Mk 2, Mk 3, Mk 5 and Mk 7 flying boats entered commercial service either with BOAC from 1946 onwards, flying to Singapore, Sydney and on the Dragon route to Hong Kong or with airlines in Argentina, Australia, New Zealand, Norway and Uruguay. Whilst the Sunderland lineage was obvious, the Sandringham was an improvement on earlier civil conversions as it featured a pleasantly streamlined nose and tail cone. The company's sales brochure waxed lyrical, "Each cabin has been designed to give

the greatest possible comfort, combined with a generous allowance of space in all gangways, thus enabling all passengers to move about with ease. The deep and well-sprung seats are fitted with adjustable head rests. Magazine or handbag pockets relieve the passenger of the miscellaneous small articles usually required for long journeys. Individual tables and glass holders for liquid refreshment are available to each passenger. Ash trays are fitted to each seat, as smoking can safely be permitted in all cabins when airborne." There was also an upper deck cocktail and snack bar, "completely fitted with

The promenade and lounge of a Sandringham. *(Bombardier Belfast)*

Author Ernie Cromie on the flightdeck of Sunderland ML814 VH-BRF. *(Ernie Cromie Collection)*

Sandringham 4 VP-LVE. *(Bombardier Belfast)*

shelves, cupboards, racks and counter. Provision is also made for the mounting of suitable Thermos Food Containers. The whole of this compartment is beautifully finished in polished wood, the carpets and the trimmings blending with the surroundings." There was more, "Opposite to the bar, there is a settee for five persons, access to the lower deck being by means of a companion way suitably carpeted and provided with handrails." Two versions were offered either with Bristol Pegasus or Pratt and Whitney Twin Wasp engines. All bar one of the Sandringham conversions were carried out in Belfast. The last BOAC aircraft to land at the famous Foynes flying boat terminal in Co Limerick was Sunderland III, G-AGJO, *Honduras*, on 24 March 1946. One Belfast-built, converted, 43-passenger Sunderland, VH-BRF, *Islander*, flew commercial passenger services from Sydney the 450 miles to Lord Howe Island until 15 August 1974. This aircraft is now owned by Kermit Weeks at Fantasy of Flight in Florida and is registered N814ML.

Test flying the BOAC Solent *Seaforth* on 31 March 1949. *(Bombardier Belfast)*

The 'Charm Room' on board a Solent. *(Bombardier Belfast)*

Engine run of the first TEAL Solent, ZK-AML on 13 April 1949. *(Bombardier Belfast)*

The S.45 Seaford was a military development of the Sunderland overtaken by the cessation of hostilities. Twelve were adapted for BOAC under the designation Solent 2; G-AHIY, *Southsea* – the final aircraft constructed at Rochester – being launched on 8 April 1948. Six more were converted to Solent 3s while under construction in Belfast, the first of which, G-AKNO, flew to Limehouse Reach on 5 May 1949 to be christened *City of London*. The Solent 3s were powered by four 1690 hp Bristol Hercules engines, had a top speed of 212 knots and a range of 1400 miles. The Springbok service to South Africa was initiated by Solent G-AHIN *Southampton* in May 1948, via Marseilles, Sicily, Cairo, Lake Victoria and Victoria Falls – a 4½ day aerial voyage which was a byword for luxury. The Solents also operated the BOAC routes to Nairobi and to Karachi, however the Corporation ceased all flying boat services on 10 November 1950. Four new Solent 4s were built in Belfast for Tasman Empire Airways Ltd (TEAL) to fly on the ocean crossing from Auckland to Sydney. The company sales brochure described the interior as follows,

"This is a long-range civil flying boat seating 34–44 passengers in a superlative degree of comfort. It has such refinements as a cocktail bar, promenade, gentlemen's dining room (with electric razor points) and a beautifully appointed ladies' powder room". The Solent's two decks were connected by a spiral staircase, the well-appointed galley on the upper deck featured electric cookers and refrigerators, while the entire aircraft was air-conditioned. The Solent 4 had a crew of seven, consisting of the Captain, Second Pilot, Navigator, Radio Operator, Engineer, Steward and Stewardess. The final UK-based company to operate the Solent was Aquila Airways, which ceased its service to Madeira on 30 September 1958, with the return of Solent 4, G-ANYI, to Southampton, thus bringing the era of British commercial flying boat activity to a close. TEAL continued to fly a single example, ZK-AMO, *Aranui*, on the Coral Route from Auckland to Fiji, Samoa, the Cook Islands and Tahiti until 1960. Two Solents are preserved, G-AKNP at the Oakland Aviation Museum in California and ZK-AMO at the Museum of Transport and Technology, Auckland.

Muriel Hambrook presents her bouquet to Princess Elizabeth. *(Bombardier Belfast)*

Right: The cover of the house journal Short Story describing the Royal Visit on 26 May 1949. *(Bombardier Belfast)*

Far right: Princess Elizabeth and the Duke of Edinburgh disembark from the Solent 4 ZK-AML Aotearoa II at Sydenham. *(Bombardier Belfast)*

The scene at Sydenham. *(Bombardier Belfast)*

On 26 May 1949 Their Royal Highnesses Princess Elizabeth and Prince Philip, Duke of Edinburgh visited Belfast. Having received the Freedom of the City of Belfast, they were driven to Queen's Island. On arrival at Shorts, the Princess was presented with a bouquet by six-year-old Muriel Hambrook, the daughter of Bill Hambrook, the Sales Controller. After passing along the Sealand production line, the Royal Party walked through the 300 foot bay, with "military Sunderlands, Sandringhams for the Argentine and Norway and Solents for BOAC and TEAL on each hand". Following a comprehensive tour of the factory, which was gaily decorated in coloured bunting, Princess Elizabeth christened the TEAL Solent 4, ZK-AML, *Aotearoa II* with a bottle of Australian wine.

The sad end of the Shetland. (*Bombardier Belfast*)

One of the proposed interior layouts for the civil version of the Shetland. (*Bombardier Belfast*)

SHORT CIVIL SHETLAND.
GENERAL ARRANGEMENT OF INTERIOR - 34 DAY PASSENGERS.
SHORT BROS LTD ROCHESTER
DRG. No BR 1524

The Short Shetland, G-AGVD, prepares to alight on Belfast Lough on 26 September 1947. (*Bombardier Belfast*)

The Short S.40 Shetland II, G-AGVD, was fitted out for carrying passengers but never entered revenue service. The interior was capable of configuration for up to 70 passengers in a high standard of comfort, with space also being allocated to a dining saloon/lounge for 12 persons and a cocktail bar on the upper deck. The flight deck accommodated a crew of five, pilot, co-pilot, navigator, radio operator and engineer. It was powered by four 2625 hp Bristol Centaurus engines and had a maximum empty weight of 34 tons, a top speed of 267 mph and a range of 4230 miles. It was the biggest British aircraft ever built when it was produced but time had passed it by, there was no market for giant flying boats either in civil or military guise. A production contract for 10 of the military version to be built in Belfast was cancelled in 1944, the first prototype, DX166, had made its initial flight at Rochester on 14 December 1944 but was burnt out at its moorings in January 1946. G-AGVD was constructed at Rochester but flown to Belfast on 25 September 1947 to complete fitting out. Proposals for operation by BOAC and later by Aquila Airways in the Berlin Airlift, then finally as an engine test-bed, did not come to fruition. Sadly, it was scrapped in 1950.

Ju-52 G-AHOF at Croydon Airport.
(Richard Riding Collection)

A Ju-52 at Shorts in September
1946. *(Bombardier Belfast)*

Conversion work was also undertaken on two civil landplane types. Firstly, the Junkers Ju-52/3m – brought over from Germany as war reparations – of which ten out of 24 delivered to Belfast between January and April 1946 were refurbished by Shorts (G-AHOC/L) with a smart royal blue interior and seating for 17 passengers. The first intimation received by Shorts was a telephone call from the Associated Airways Joint Committee in December 1945, asking if the company would be interested in taking on this work. Early in the New Year the Ministry of Aircraft Production rang to say that a contract was on its way. The cost of each conversion was between £10,000 and £12,500. Known as the Jupiter class, the service to Belfast from Croydon via Liverpool was inaugurated by G-AHOG on 18 November 1946 by Railway Air Services on behalf of British European Airways. Despite being easy to fly, light on the controls, sedate and having the capability to lift a good payload, this type

had only limited success, chiefly due to a lack of useable spares. Moreover, they had been constructed during the war to much lower standards than pre-war machines, in the realistic expectation of a much shorter active life. It also had an unfortunate tendency to shed its nose engine cowling in flight and more than once, the airline's office received a call from an irate inhabitant or two of Co Down who had literally found a foreign object in their field. The famous aviation author and historian, AJ Jackson, described the aircraft thus, "The cabin had been furnished in a light and artistic decor with airline seats complete with folding tables, and there was a toilet compartment in the rear which still boasted a light switch marked 'Ein' and 'Aus'. The breakfast of sandwiches, biscuits and hot coffee was more than welcome in view of a serious malfunction in the cabin heating system." They were withdrawn from service in 1948 and scrapped.

The Halton's cabin looking to the rear. *(Bombardier Belfast)*

The Halton G-AHDU, *Falkirk*, with an Avro Lancaster in the background. *(Bombardier Belfast)*

Secondly, 12 Handley Page Halifax C.8 transports were converted into Halton Is for BOAC. This was a stop-gap measure due to delays affecting production of the Avro Tudor. Seating for 12 passengers was provided and small rectangular windows were added to illuminate the cabin. The glazed nose was replaced by metal skin, with the compartment being used for the carriage of freight, to which could be added the 8000 lbs capacity of the ventral pannier. The first Halton I was G-AHDU *Falkirk*, it entered service in September 1946. The type was mostly used on the routes to West Africa and London – Cairo – Karachi. By the end of 1947, BOAC began to replace the Haltons with Canadair DC-4Ms, though 11 of the Haltons gained an extra lease of life during the Berlin Airlift in 1948–9 flying for Bond Air Services, Skyflight, the Lancashire Aircraft Corporation

and Eagle Aviation. One aircraft, G-AHDL, crashed in Germany on 1 April 1949. A typical load would have been six and a half tons of flour or coal. The last civil flight made during the Airlift was made on 15 August 1949 by a Halton of Eagle Aviation. By 1950 most of the Haltons had been scrapped, the last one, G-AHDV, flew for the Lancashire Aircraft Corporation until December 1952, when it was damaged beyond repair during a gale at Blackpool Airport. A further contract required the conversion of two Halifax for Compagnie Africane de Travail Aerien; only one aircraft, PP238, was received and served briefly with the French Air Force before ending up as G-AJZY with the Lancashire Aircraft Corporation and being lost in a crash in 1951.

Rear Admiral Matthew Slattery before a flight in the Nimbus. *(Bombardier Belfast)*

The Nimbus in flight. *(Bombardier Belfast)*

Two members of the Gliding Club prepare for a flight in 1950. *(Bombardier Belfast)*

A unique type which was constructed in Rochester, the last Shorts' aircraft to be wholly designed and built there, and brought to Belfast after the Company's change of location in 1947, was the Nimbus high-performance glider, which was given the construction number S.1312 and was registered BGA470. It was a tandem two-seater, chiefly made of spruce, plywood and fabric, with a perspex canopy. It gave many years of faithful service to members of the Shorts Gliding Club at Sydenham from 1949 (though it was officially opened in June 1950) and then at Bishops Court and Maghaberry until it was damaged in an accident in 1956. Semi-restored, it was gifted to the London Gliding Club in 1969 and within a year it was flying again from Dunstable. It was later based at RAF St Mawgan and flew in the National Gliding Championships at Bicester in 1974. It is now with the Ulster Folk and Transport Museum, which acquired the Nimbus in 1985.

Sturgeon TT Mk 2, TS488. (*Bombardier Belfast*)

The Sturgeon Mk 1 on 18 May 1948.
(*Bombardier Belfast*)

Sea trials for the Sturgeon on board
HMS *Illustrious* in 1950. (*Bombardier Belfast*)

The S.38 Sturgeon was originally intended as a reconnaissance-torpedo-bomber but with the construction of new aircraft carriers suspended at the end of the war, the requirement no longer existed. It was the first twin-engine aircraft designed expressly to a Royal Naval specification for carrier operations and was intended for the projected *Ark Royal* and *Hermes* classes. The first prototype, RK787, made its maiden flight in 1946 at Rochester in the hands of Geoffrey Tyson. It was powered by a pair of 1440 hp Merlin engines driving contra-rotating propellers. The second prototype was the Sturgeon 1, RK791, which flew from Sydenham on 18 May 1948. Both carried out carrier landing trials, on HMS *Illustrious* and HMS *Implacable* respectively. These were followed by the prototype Mk 2, VR363, under the designations S.39 and subsequently SA.2. It formed the basis for the main production model, the TT Mk 2, of which 23 entered service with the Royal Navy, fully equipped for deck-landing, with power-operated folding wings and a lengthened nose to accommodate photographic equipment. They flew from aircraft carriers for Fleet gunnery practice, air-to-air firing exercises, photographic marking and radar calibration. The Sturgeon target tug began sea trials aboard HMS *Illustrious* in June 1950. Nineteen of these were subsequently modified to TT Mk 3, land-based standard, reverting to the short nose of the original aircraft, had manually folding wings and from which the deck-landing gear was deleted. They subsequently performed usefully, towing winged or sleeved targets for ship-to-air and air-to-air firing, flying with 728 Naval Air Squadron from Malta amongst other bases. On sorties, two aircraft were routinely used, one acting as a camera ship to record the results. The Sturgeon was withdrawn from service in 1958, being superseded by Gloster Meteor TT 20s.

The SB.3 could not be described as a handsome design. *(Bombardier Belfast)*

The unique Sturgeon SB.3, which was displayed at the Farnborough Air Show in 1950. *(Bombardier Belfast)*

The final development of the Sturgeon was the SB.3, WF632, a competitor for the Fairey Gannet in the anti-submarine role. It was powered by two Armstrong Siddeley Mamba turboprops and first flew on 12 August 1950 in the hands of Tom Brooke-Smith (who had taken over as Chief Test Pilot from Pip Piper in 1948 and who was to remain in post for the next 12 years). It was a deeply ugly looking machine with a bulbous nose, which provided the accommodation for a search radar and two operators. It made an appearance that year at the Farnborough Show and carried out flight testing in 1951 but by the end of the year had been broken up for spares. It is also significant in that this was a half-way house to building aircraft completely designed in Belfast, rather than Rochester, as it was a Northern Ireland-designed conversion of a Rochester-built aeroplane. It was also the first Shorts gas-turbine powered aircraft to fly.

The Sealand's passenger compartment. *(Bombardier Belfast)*

Cover of a Sealand sales brochure. *(Bombardier Belfast)*

Sealand G-AKLU flies along the shoreline by Strangford Lough in 1950. *(Bombardier Belfast)*

The maiden flight of the first SA.6 Sealand amphibian, G-AIVX, was on 22 January 1948, with Pip Piper at the controls. This was the first new aircraft to fly at Belfast since the completion of the final Sunderland in May 1946. Having been designed jointly by the Rochester and Belfast design offices, it was also the first Short prototype to make its maiden flight from Queen's Island. It was a very elegant and attractive aircraft and was intended for a variety of roles – charter work for both freight and passengers, feeder liner, VIP transport, air ambulance – to name a few. It could carry between five and eight passengers and was powered by two 340 hp Gipsy Queen engines. The fourth example off the production line, G-AKLP, completed a 50,000 miles sales tour of North and South America in 1951, including a double crossing of the Andes. Twenty-four were built (of which 12 were constructed at the Altona factory in Lisburn) one was delivered to Egypt, two to Borneo, two to Indonesia, two to Norway, three to Pakistan, one to Venezuela, two to Yugoslavia and ten to the Indian Navy. The first production aircraft was lost in a crash in September 1949 while on a sales tour of Sweden. The first Indian aircraft was delivered in January 1953, this batch having uprated engines, dual controls and extra fuel tanks. The sales

Nadia is handed over to the owner's personal pilot, Captain S Omar. *(Bombardier Belfast)*

Sealand G-AKLO at Gibraltar in 1950 during a sales tour which covered 8000 miles, 150 flying hours and 50 sales demonstrations in Europe, North Africa and the Canary Islands. *(Bombardier Belfast)*

Sealand being moved from Extension Factory to Flight and Service hangar, November 1947. *(Bombardier Belfast)*

brochure devoted a page to water handling skills and proclaimed the advantages of one-man operations, "Taxi the aircraft so that the buoy passes close to the cockpit on the starboard side. Using the short boathook provided, engage the strop of the buoy, then, sliding back starboard window fully, step out onto the special ledge, open nose hatch, enclosing mooring gear, and make aircraft fast to the mooring bollard". It also noted, "Smoking is permitted, ash-trays being supplied at convenient points." The Sealand's sales prospects were not helped by the ready availability of US amphibians such as the Grumman G-21 Goose and G-44 Widgeon, of which more than 600 were sold. The prototype was used as a company hack until 1954,

often with the wing floats and struts removed for land operations only. One example, SU-AHY (G-AKLW), survives in Northern Ireland. It was delivered in February 1952 to His Excellency Ahmed Abboud Pasha, the director of the Khedival Mail Line of Cairo and named after his daughter, Nadia. It boasted a luxury fit of six blue, leather seats, along with a bookcase and wine rack. It is currently under restoration in the Ulster Folk and Transport Museum. Two others have been preserved, 662 at the Aeronautical Museum, Nicola Tesla Airport, Belgrade and IN106 in the Indian Fleet Air Arm Museum at Dabolim in Goa.

Both Sperrins in formation. *(Bombardier Belfast)*

The Sperrin was an imposing size.
(Bombardier Belfast)

The prototype SA.4 Sperrin four-jet, heavy bomber, VX158, flown by Chief Test Pilot, Tom Brooke-Smith, took to the air on 10 August 1951 at Aldergrove. This was followed by VX161 which had its maiden flight on 12 August 1952 in the hands of Wally Runciman and Malcolm Wild the Flight Test Development Engineer. Shorts were asked to build an aircraft which, while possessing relatively high performance, would not be unduly unorthodox in its general layout. It was an insurance policy against the possible failure of the Vickers Valiant the first of the 'V-Bombers'. Despite having very little wing sweepback, external, easily accessible, podded engines and manual servo tab flying controls, it had very similar capabilities to the Valiant, which was much delayed in development and later suffered in-service fatigue life problems. One particularly interesting feature of the Sperrin was the pressurised compartment for the five crew members, pilot, co-pilot, navigator, bomb aimer and radio operator. It was powered by four Rolls-Royce Avon engines, which gave it good performance at high level. It was capable of delivering up to 20,000 lbs of bombs, with a cruising speed of 564 mph and

Sperrin VX158, the test aircraft for the Gyron engine, at RAF Aldergrove. *(Bombardier Belfast)*

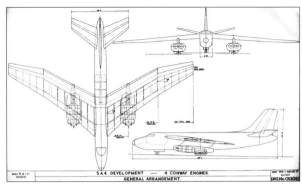

The design for a Sperrin with an aero-isoclinic wing. *(Bombardier Belfast)*

The wind tunnel at Sydenham in 1956. *(Bombardier Belfast)*

a maximum range of 3860 miles (with a 10,000 lb payload). Sadly both Sperrins were scrapped before the end of the decade, after giving useful service as flying test-beds for the V-bomber radar blind-bombing system, the de Havilland Gyron engine and the development of a British nuclear weapon. The work of the design team at Shorts, which was recognised by the Ministry of Supply as having "the promise of becoming exceptionally good", would have been assisted by the provision of a high speed wind tunnel, which eventually became operational in 1956, having earlier been seized from Blohm and Voss in Hamburg as war reparations. Freighter and troop carrying versions of the Sperrin were studied, as was an aero-isoclinic derivative. David Keith-Lucas proposed that this latter concept should be trialled using a contemporary Hawker or Supermarine fighter, the Ministry of Supply suggested converting the SB.5. However none of the ideas progressed any further.

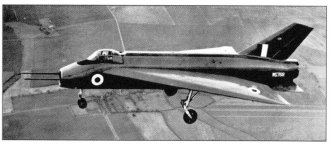

SB.5 WG768 flying near Bedford with a low tail and 69 degrees sweep-back on 18 October 1960. *(Bombardier Belfast)*

Company test pilot Alex Roberts in the SB.5 in November 1960. *(Bombardier Belfast)*

The SB.5 in flight. *(Bombardier Belfast)*

The SB.5 experimental research aircraft, WG 768, carried out its maiden flight, flown by Tom Brooke-Smith, on 2 December 1952 at Boscombe Down. Over the course of the test and trial period its wing was re-configured from 50, to 60 and finally 69 degrees, embodying a greater sweepback than any other British aircraft of the period. Another unusual feature was that two rear fuselage and tailplane sections were constructed, one with the tailplane on top of the fin and the other with it beneath the fuselage, these were interchangeable during the test programme. It was powered by a single Rolls-Royce Derwent engine and was designed for experiments in control at low speeds. It was the first aircraft to come from the Keith-Lucas team of designers and was designed at the request of the Ministry of Supply to be "as like the aircraft being designed by English Electric to Specification F23/49 as possible". The results of the flying investigations carried out by the SB.5 were made available to the whole of the British aircraft industry, "for the benefit of British aviation" as the company magazine noted. Brooke-Smith also performed a very impressive display in the SB.5 at the Farnborough Air Show in 1953 and "made it appear so versatile in the air that one could scarcely believe that it was designed for experiments in control

at low speeds, while his impressive breakaways demonstrated a manoeuvrability that belied its appearance." Later it was based at RAE Bedford, where a new engine was installed, the Bristol Orpheus and also a Martin-Baker ejection seat, for the 69 degree sweep part of the trials, which began in October 1960; the initial flight being made by Denis Tayler. It made an important contribution to the English Electric P.1 programme, the first British aircraft to exceed the speed of sound in level flight, which resulted ultimately in the Lightning (which itself had a wing sweepback of 69 degrees). The SB.5 was effectively a 7/8th low speed, scale model of the P.1A (which flew for the first time on 4 August 1954). One of the important concepts which it proved was that the lower tailplane position preferred by English Electric was more suitable than the T-tail favoured by RAE Farnborough. The English Electric Chief Test Pilot, Roly Beaumont, flew the SB.5 no less than 23 times. After completion of the flight test programme the aircraft served with the Empire Test Pilots School at Boscombe Down between 1965 and 1967, to give students experience in testing 'slender aircraft'. The SB.5 is today part of the collection at the Royal Air Force Museum, Cosford.

A wreath is dropped into the sea.
(via Jan Edmunds)

Rev AL Melrose conducting a service in the Sunderland flying boat over the scene of the disaster. The RAF officer is Flight Lieutenant Ben Ford, the others are Shorts' representatives. *(via Jan Edmunds)*

A dreadful accident at sea, which affected the whole company, occurred on Saturday 31 January 1953, with the sinking of Larne-Stranraer ferry, the SS *Princess Victoria*. In all 128 lives were lost, including 16 Shorts' employees, some with their wives and children. The company magazine, *Short Story,* noted, "This tragedy has shocked the entire nation, but particularly has its impact been felt in Northern Ireland. There can be few who, if not actually relatives, did not know some of those who lost their lives." An emergency committee was swiftly formed from members of the management, which met at the factory that same evening and made every effort to assist the bereaved and the eight members of staff who survived. On 5 February that year, a Short Sunderland flew over the site of the disaster and dropped wreaths on behalf of the RAF, Stranraer Town Council and the Company. The inscription attached to the RAF's wreath stated, "We who relied upon their skill, salute them and deeply regret being unable to help them when they needed us most."

The Seamew production line, note the Britannias in the background. *(Bombardier Belfast)*

An attractive colour image of a Seamew. *(Bombardier Belfast)*

The SB.6 Seamew was a rather quaint looking aeroplane. It was intended as a lightweight turboprop anti-submarine aircraft. The prototype, XA209, first flew on 23 August 1953 and made its debut at Farnborough the same year. The test pilot on both occasions was Squadron Leader WJ 'Wally' Runciman DFM, AFC, another New Zealander, who had flown Stirlings during the war. The philosophy behind its design was described in the *Shorts Quarterly Review*, "The continued tendency for military aircraft of all types to grow larger and more complicated is creating an immense economic problem of increasing importance to those countries forming the North Atlantic Treaty Organisation. Somehow this trend has got to be checked. Within the last ten years aircraft have trebled their weight and costs have soared. For each unit of additional weight a larger wing is needed to lift it, a larger fuel tank is needed to feed the engine and to hold all this a more solid structure is essential." Thirty were ordered for the Royal Navy, the AS Mk 1, and the same number of a land-based version for RAF Coastal Command, the MR Mk 2. Carrier deck landing trials were carried out on board HMS *Bulwark* (also constructed in Belfast) in November 1955. The RAF order was cancelled in February 1956, even though the first MR2, XE173, had already flown. Later that year a formation of four Seamews performed at Farnborough. It was designed to a Government specification for

Flight magazine featured the Seamew on its cover in February 1956. (via *(Bombardier Belfast)*)

A Seamew approaches HMS *Bulwark* to land in 1955. *(Bombardier Belfast)*

Wally Runciman is on the right on board HMS *Bulwark* in December 1955. *(Bombardier Belfast)*

operation from small carriers, dictating slow approach speeds, with crisp handling but at the same time having the structural strength for relatively high diving speeds for submarine attack. The range of speed from 48 to 300 knots made it very difficult for the aerodynamic and flight test personnel to develop the manual flight controls to give light handling at low carrier approach speeds while 'heavying up' at increasing speed to prevent excess control application and aircraft break up, while maintaining high maneuverability in the dive attack role. According to Malcolm Wild, "To the test fraternity it was like playing with a king size, albeit very expensive, model aeroplane.

rather hard on the flight test engineers' stomachs!" The Seamew had a crew of two and was powered by an Armstrong Siddeley Mamba turboprop. It could carry up to 1844 lbs of stores including sonobuoys and depth-charges. As a weight saving measure, it had a fixed undercarriage. Sadly the company test pilot, Wally Runciman, was killed at the age of 35 on 9 June 1956 while flying the Seamew XE175 at the RAFA display at Sydenham. Only a small number had been accepted by the Royal Navy when the project was cancelled, falling victim to the Treasury's axe in 1957. In all, 24 Seamews were constructed.

A Straddle Carrier, Shorland armoured car and aircraft passenger seats manufactured by Shorts. *(Bombardier Belfast)*

Matthew Slattery with models of the Seamew and SB.5. *(Bombardier Belfast)*

The aim with the Seamew was to provide the RN with larger numbers of cheaper aircraft. One of the prime movers behind this idea was Rear Admiral Matthew Slattery CB, DSC, the Chairman and Managing Director of Shorts, who had also been the Director General of Naval Aircraft Development and Production. He was first appointed to the Board of the Company in 1948, becoming in due course Managing Director and then Chairman in 1952. He received a knighthood in 1955. His influence on the company was immense during his 12 years of dedicated service. He encouraged the diversification which ensured the survival of the company during a difficult decade. Other work included the manufacture of passenger seats for the Vickers Viscount airliner and the RAF's Armstrong

A display of Shorts' carpet sweepers at Olympia in February 1965. *(Bombardier Belfast)*

The aluminium-built Hillfoot Restaurant. *(Bombardier Belfast)*

The Shorland Conveyancer of 1962. *(Bombardier Belfast)*

Nobel 200 production in 1960. *(Bombardier Belfast)*

Whitworth Argosy; Nobel 200 two-passenger, three-wheeler cars, the Shorland Straddle Carriers and fork-lift trucks; aluminium frame buildings, which included schools and hospitals; milk churns, wringers, bathroom cabinets and the Mercury – Merlin, Meteor, Midas and Mermaid carpet sweepers. (It is historically interesting to note that the same problem had faced Shorts at Rochester after the end of the First World War, diversification in the 1920s included thousands of bus and tram bodies, mooring buoys, prams, children's pedal cycles and bus conductors' ticket punches).

The flight simulator in operation.
(Bombardier Belfast)

The first production line of analogue computers in the British Isles was at Castlereagh. *(Thales Belfast)*

The analogue computer developed by the Precision Engineering Division at Castlereagh was a rather more technically advanced project. Shorts exhibited it at Farnborough in 1953 and over the next few years some 72 were sold at a price of £5300 each. One purchaser apparently regarded the computer with 'no particular enthusiasm' but was delighted with the ingenious design work involved in incorporating an integral, retractable, chrome-plated ash tray. The Design Office also used several of the computers as an aid to the Company's test pilots, coupling two together, linking them to a dummy cockpit to produce a flight simulator. These ventures into advanced electronics were the start of a highly successful and profitable new line of business, which would eventually spawn a highly successful range of guided missiles.

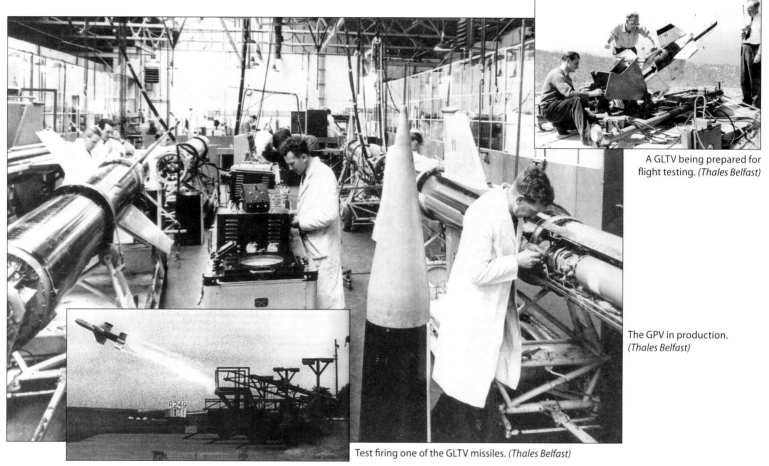

A GLTV being prepared for flight testing. *(Thales Belfast)*

The GPV in production. *(Thales Belfast)*

Test firing one of the GLTV missiles. *(Thales Belfast)*

The Royal Navy was interested in a low-cost missile to replace the Bofors gun. Shorts began studying the proposition with the General Purpose Vehicle (GPV) supersonic, radar-guided missile, which tested propulsion, guidance and control systems, telemetry and instrumentation. Forty GPVs were built from the time of its first launch in 1953. An example went on show to the public for the first time at the Company's stand at Farnborough. Almost all of the GPVs were fired at the Aberporth Range in Wales, one example is preserved in the Science Museum in London. In 1956 Shorts gained the contract to research a short-range, anti-aircraft (AA) missile.

This was the Green Light Test Vehicle (GLTV) which was manually controlled by means of a joystick with a thumb button and visually guided by the operator monitoring its flight through high-power binoculars. Twelve GLTVs were built and 11 of these were launched. The experience gained designing, building, testing and flight-testing the GPV and the GLTV gave Castlereagh the expertise to progress in the guided weapons field. Its selected niche was the close-range AA missile with a range of up to 6 km to defend ships or a land-based military installation.

Short SB.4 Sherpa over County Antrim.
(Bombardier Belfast)

The SB.4 Sherpa near the shoreline of Lough Neagh. *(Bombardier Belfast)*

The SB.4 Sherpa (G-14-1) which took to the air on 4 October 1953 at Aldergrove, flown by Tom Brooke-Smith, two months after the first flight of the Seamew, had an aero-isoclinic wing – the principle was that instead of the wing being as stiff as possible, it was relatively flexible and able to distort in an 'advantageous manner'. Instead of conventional ailerons or elevators, the aircraft was provided with all moving wing-tips, comprising approximately one fifth of the total wing area, which could be rotated either together or in opposition. It was a small, single-seat, tail-less aeroplane and was powered by two Blackburn Turboméca Palas turbojets of 350 lbs thrust each,

which were started and shut down from a small auxiliary tank of AVGAS, switching to AVTUR for the flight. While not being capable of high speed itself, the intention of the research programme was to investigate problems associated with the design of swept wings for future high-speed civil and military aircraft. Tom Brooke-Smith conducted the early trial flights and pronounced it to be, "one of the most graceful aircraft now flying". It had an endurance of about half an hour, 'Jock' Eassie did most of the test flying as he was the lightest pilot. Malcolm Wild recalls, "On one occasion the aircraft went out of sight after landing and after a long wait duly appeared

David Keith-Lucas, Matthew Slattery and Tom Brooke-Smith admire a model of the SB.4. *(Bombardier Belfast)*

Professor Geoffrey Hill. *(Bombardier Belfast)*

The SB.1 in flight – note the towing cable. *(Bombardier Belfast)*

with Jock pushing it!" It was developed from the full re-design and re-build of the SB.1 glider, G-14-5, which had flown from Aldergrove on 14 July 1951, having been winch launched. The private venture SB.1 was the first Short aircraft to be wholly designed in Northern Ireland. Tom Brooke-Smith proposed that a Sturgeon would be a suitable tug for the glider. A fortnight later it was towed aloft behind the Sturgeon TT Mk 2, VR363, flown by Jock Eassie. On the second flight of the day the buffeting created by the slipstream of the Sturgeon caused the SB.1 to crash, injuring Brooke-Smith severely. This hastened the decision to fit engines. Both aircraft

were the work of the Chief Designer, David Keith-Lucas and also of Professor Geoffrey Hill, they gave much valuable research data. The SB.1 was actually a one third scale model of a preliminary design by Keith-Lucas for an advanced jet bomber, the PD.1. The SB.4 was flown at Cranfield College of Aeronautics between 1957 and 1964 and is now part of the Ulster Aviation Collection at Maze/Long Kesh (minus its wing, which is presently a reconstruction project). David Keith-Lucas came to Belfast from Rochester in 1945 and worked there for the next 20 years, successively as Chief Aerodynamicist, Chief Designer, Technical Director and Research Director.

Cocooned North American Sabres at Shorts. *(Bombardier Belfast)*

Comet production at Shorts in 1954. *(Bombardier Belfast)*

As well as constructing its own designs for naval aircraft, flying boats, amphibians and research aircraft, Shorts gained much needed work by licence agreements with other manufacturers. The de Havilland Company decided in 1952 to open up a second production line in Belfast for the Comet, the world's first jet airliner. Over 1600 personnel were engaged in work related to this contract and two complete fuselages had been shipped to Chester when it was suspended, never to be renewed, in 1954, after the terrible series of crashes which badly affected its commercial prospects. The company was compensated to a small extent by building wing spars for later versions of the aircraft. The loss of the work on the Comet was a blow to Shorts, as was the relative lack of success enjoyed by the Supermarine Swift jet fighter, as compared to the Hawker

Hunter. If the Swift had been a resounding triumph, the company was poised to take on a considerable amount of collaborative work. Indeed jigs had already been built in the factory. As partial compensation the company received 'fill-in' contracts between 1955 and 1956 to de-cocoon and prepare for flight 93 North American Harvards and 161 F-86 Sabres delivered from US stocks as part of a Western European re-armament programme, as well as processing and dispatching 140 F-86s to the States via the USS *Tripoli* and USS *Corregidor*, moored at Airport Wharf. It is reported that the Company Production Manager came to blows with a USAF officer over "a matter of contract interpretation", which may possibly have been why it was a long time before Shorts had any further dealings with the USAF!

The maiden flight of Canberra B.2 WH853 on 30 October 1952. *(Bombardier Belfast)*

Front port view of U Mk 10 WJ987 lifting off at Sydenham with landing gear still retracting. *(Bombardier Belfast)*

The Canberra production line at Shorts in March 1954. *(Bombardier Belfast)*

A welcome long-term partnership was established on 30 October 1950, when the Company was contracted to produce English Electric Canberras. This was part of a super priority contract brought about by Britain's Cold War re-armament programme and stimulated further by North Korea's invasion of South Korea in June 1950. The first Belfast built Canberra B2, WH853, made its maiden flight on 30 October 1952 in the hands the Company's Chief Test Pilot, Tom Brooke-Smith – four years later it dropped the first bombs of the Suez campaign in the attack on Almaza airfield in Egypt on 31 October 1956. Shorts built more Canberras for the RAF than any other manufacturer apart from the parent company – 60 B2s, 49 B6s, 12 B(I)8s and 23 PR9s, as well as converting 24 B2s to U10 pilotless target drones for use at the Woomera Weapons Range in Australia and six of these to improved SC6/D14 configuration for the Royal Navy to use in ship-to-air missile trials. The U10 used electrical components for its control system, whereas the D14 had a hydraulic system, the Precision Engineering Division at Castlereagh being heavily involved in the design of both conversions, as a spin-off from its work on command-link guided missiles.

Britannias being built in Belfast in November 1957.
(Bombardier Belfast)

The Britannia's flightdeck.
(via Dick Spencer)

At the end of 1953 an agreement was made between Shorts and the Bristol Company to build Britannia turboprop airliners. Bristols also acquired a 15¼ per cent interest in Shorts. On 2 June 1955, Britannia, G-ANBB, in BOAC livery, landed at Sydenham airfield "the largest aircraft ever to land there" bringing a delegation from Bristols. The first to be constructed in Belfast flew on 1 June 1957 "a few minutes before 5.00 pm the first Belfast-built Britannia, for Northeast

Airlines of Boston, set off with a resounding hum of turbines and rose sweetly into the air. People looked up to see the 'Whispering Giant' wheel and bank above their heads as it turned back towards Sydenham. There, pilot Ken Ashley from Bristol indulged in a mild beat-up before once again climbing away to set course for Filton." In the event, Northeast Airlines cancelled its order but other buyers were found. The first military Britannia flew on 13 October 1958,

Loading a Britannia through the forward cargo door. Note the air-portable freight lift specially designed by Shorts. *(Bombardier Belfast)*

The first Britannia to be built in Belfast makes its maiden flight on 1 June 1957. *(Bombardier Belfast)*

A very striking image of a Britannia at Shorts. *(Bombardier Belfast)*

two variants were produced – three Type 252 C.2s, which were equipped to civil standards and were primarily for trooping and 20 Type 253 C.1s, which had a fully strengthened freight floor. These were all powered by four Bristol Proteus engines. They gave excellent service with Numbers 99 and 511 Squadrons until withdrawn as part of a round of defence cuts in 1975. In all, 12 civil and 18 military Britannias were constructed in Belfast (out of a total of 85). Shorts also supplied major components to the Bristol civil production line and for five RAF aircraft assembled at Filton. The type never achieved the commercial success that was anticipated, the Boeing 707 and DC-8 had arrived on the scene and captured much of the potential market. Nevertheless it was well-loved by passengers and aircrews alike. The last airworthy Britannia, currently in retirement at Cotswold Airport, is a Shorts-built example, XM496 *Regulus*.

Short Seacat missiles on board HMS *Devonshire*, from an original oil painting by Raymond Piper (1923–2007). *(Bombardier Belfast)*

Seacat components in production. *(Bombardier Belfast)*

The Seacat Team, Philip Foreman is standing on the far right. *(Bombardier Belfast)*

Work on the Seacat GWS-20 close-range, anti-aircraft system – missile, launcher and director – got under way in 1956. A production site was set up at Queen's Island and the first Seacat production contract for the RN was agreed in 1957. Shorts built the electronics, airframe, wings, control and guidance systems, as well as the test equipment. The fuse, motor and warhead were outsourced. The whole package was then assembled in Royal Naval Armament Depots. One of the engineers working on the project was Philip Foreman, who had been recruited from the Admiralty Research Establishment, Teddington. His work there on the Seacat launcher had come to the notice of Shorts' Chief Engineer, Hugh Conway (Joint Managing Director 1961–64), who persuaded him to join the company and come to Belfast in October 1958 to look after the design and development of all the shipborne and armament depot equipment associated with Seacat.

Above and top right: The rocket sled in action on
the test track at Langford Lodge. *(Martin-Baker)*

Irishman and ejection seat test ejectee, Bernard
Lynch (left) and Sir James Martin. *(Martin-Baker)*

Meanwhile, in England in 1920, Ulsterman James Martin had founded a small engineering business which grew and diversified, and in 1934 became the Martin-Baker Aircraft Company. During the Second World War, the company designed and produced impressive quantities of armament and aircraft-related equipment and by the 1950s it was receiving orders for a novel product with which its name is still universally associated – aircraft ejection seats – and Martin was seeking to bring some aspects of that business to Northern Ireland. In 1958, the disused wartime airfield at Langford Lodge was acquired for the purpose of setting up a sub-contractor, Langford Lodge Engineering, to manufacture selected components for Martin-Baker ejection seats. The enterprise prospered and, ten years later, work commenced there on the construction of a rail track for Martin-Baker's exclusive use for the testing of their seats. Constructed to exacting standards, it is 6000 feet in length, capable of carrying a rocket-powered sled moving at speeds up to 1000 feet per second and was completed in 1970. Martin-Baker ejection seats have equipped more than 90 of the world's air forces and to date have saved the lives of almost 7500 military pilots. The new Lockheed F-35 Joint Strike Fighter being developed for supply to several countries including the UK is equipped with the Martin-Baker US16E seat. Awarded many honours in recognition of his achievements, James Martin was knighted in 1965. He died in 1981, aged 87. Langford Lodge Engineering is now part of the RLC Engineering Group and also produces precision components, sub-assemblies and high value services for the wider aerospace industry, including Martin-Baker.

The SC.1 undergoing tethered flight trials in 1958. *(Bombardier Belfast)*

The SC.1 hovers at Sydenham. *(Bombardier Belfast)*

Short SC.1. *(Bombardier Belfast)*

In the late 1950s, Shorts produced the SC.1, which was a highly important research project in the development of vertical take-off and landing (VTOL) aircraft. It was powered by five Rolls-Royce RB.108 turbojets, one in the tail for propulsion and four in the fuselage centre section for lift. After taxi trials in Belfast on 17 December 1956, the first conventional take-off was made by XG900 at Boscombe Down on 2 April 1957. The first free vertical take-off was made by XG905 (following tethered hovering trials in May of that year) and took place at Sydenham on 25 October 1958, in the capable hands of Tom Brooke-Smith. The House Journal reported, "It took off from a low level metal platform. It rose straight up to a considerable height and for a while hovered motionless. Then, under complete control, it moved forward for some distance before landing on the runway." A few days later it followed this up by landing on a football pitch near the runway. This was a deliberate experiment and resulted in, "no detrimental effect on the turf beyond a slight scorching of the grass under the central engine bay." The SC.1 was fitted with an auto-stabiliser system which proved very effective during the extended hover periods of up to seven minutes. On 6 April 1960, at RAE Bedford, it became the world's first jet aircraft to complete the transition from vertical to forward horizontal flight and vice versa, again flown by Tom Brooke-Smith. This important moment in aviation history was described as follows, "Taking off as a conventional aeroplane, Brooke-Smith flew round the circuit and

The Short SC.1 demonstrates transition from vertical to forward flight at RAE Bedford in 1960. *(Bombardier Belfast)*

The SC.1, crated as a complete airframe, is swung aboard the SS *Empire Nordic* at Sydenham in the summer of 1959, for the first stage of its journey to RAE Bedford. The aircraft was shipped to Preston, taken by road to the English Electric Company's airfield at Warton and flown from there to Bedford by Tom Brooke-Smith. *(Bombardier Belfast)*

Test pilot Dick Green.
(Bombardier Belfast)

lit the four lift engines at 160 knots. He then made a long approach to the main runway, gradually decelerating and progressively transferring the burden of supporting the aircraft from the wing to the lift engines. Complete transition was accomplished at a height of 100 feet, but Brooke-Smith continued to descend at zero forward speed until the aircraft was hovering 20 feet above the intersection of the runways. Then to complete the sequence the aircraft was accelerated forwards, using both the lift and propulsion engines and translated back into normal aeroplane flight. Brooke-Smith climbed back to the circuit and finally landed conventionally." At the Farnborough Air Show, on 5 September 1960, vertical take-off, transition, pirouettes and vertical landing were demonstrated to the

public. In May/June 1961, XG900 flew across the English Channel and back to take part in the Paris Air Show. The pilots were Denis Tayler and Alex Roberts, who alternated over the seven stages from Bedford to Le Bourget and five on the return journey. Tragically, a runaway gyro caused XG905 to crash on 2 October 1963, killing the pilot, Dick Green. The experience gained during the programme was a major contribution to the success of the famous Harrier Jump-Jet. One of these two aircraft, XG905, which was rebuilt, is on display in the Ulster Folk and Transport Museum. The other, XG900, is at the Science Museum, London, having continued to be used for VTOL research until 1971.

Mock-up of PR9 navigator's station. *(Bombardier Belfast)*

XH129 takes off from Sydenham on its maiden flight in July 1958. *(Bombardier Belfast)*

The new nose configuration in September 1959. Alex Roberts is climbing into the cockpit, John McDonald is in the nose. *(Bombardier Belfast)*

Further work came the Company's way in respect of the Canberra. This was the last new-build Canberra variant, the PR9. It had more powerful versions of the Avon engine and increased wingspan and chord to improve the high altitude performance. The first PR9, XH129, flew from Sydenham on 27 July 1958. Tragically it crashed less than three months later due to structural failure when the enlarged wing failed as its skin peeled back. The flight test observer (FTO) Mr PH Durrant of English Electric was killed. Shorts was deeply involved in the subsequent complete redesign of the nose compartment and navigator's station. In the words of former Canberra flyer, Ken Delve, "If ever a Canberra was like a fighter it was this one. The PR9 was equally happy at 450 knots at 250 feet (if a little noisy and somewhat difficult to turn) and 60,000 feet plus – immune from most air defences." The pilot sat under a fighter-style canopy, the navigator was less fortunate. He entered the aircraft via the hinged nose compartment and had no forward vision, merely two small side windows. In all, 23 were designed and built by Shorts, XH129 to 137 and XH164 to 177. The Project Development pilot was Alex Roberts,

XH132 undergoing refurbishment at Shorts. *(Bombardier Belfast)*

who flew 21 of the PR9s. The last Canberra to be worked on by Shorts was a PR9, XH134, which flew to Boscombe Down from Belfast in the autumn of 1991. A single SC9, XH132, was also taken from the production batch and specially adapted, to be used by the Royal Aircraft Establishment for missile development tasks. Canberras

still carrying out vital frontline duties in Afghanistan in June 2006 just before they were honourably retired. In 2011 the Ulster Aviation Society brought Canberra PR9, XH131, back home to Northern Ireland for display as part of the Ulster Aviation Collection at Maze Long Kesh. Further details of this may be found in *The Last Canberra*

Seacat missiles ready for dispatch.
(Bombardier Belfast)

The Seacat director and launcher on board HMS *Decoy*.
(Bombardier Belfast)

Seacat Quad launcher.
(Bombardier Belfast)

Seacat being fired from HMS *Decoy*
in 1962. *(Bombardier Belfast)*

Seacat made its Farnborough debut in 1959. Development trials then took place at Aberporth in the same year. These were followed by sea trials on board HMS *Decoy* in 1961. It was accepted into service by the RN in 1962 and also won the Queen's Award to Industry for Technical Innovation – one of many Queen's Awards to be won by Shorts. By the late 1960s Seacat was in service with 13 countries and was the world's most widely sold guided weapon system. There were four main variants, the initial GWS-20 system, the more advanced GWS-21, the GWS-22, which was ACLOS (Automatic, Command Line-of-Sight) capable and the GWS-24, which was fitted to the RN's Type 21 frigates. A Seacat launcher, along with dummy missiles is preserved at the Ulster Aviation Collection at Maze/Long Kesh.

Tom Brooke-Smith with the SB.4.
(*Bombardier Belfast*)

Tom Brooke-Smith and the SC.1. (*Cobham Archive*)

Tom Brooke-Smith retired from active flying in 1960 after 12 years as Chief Test Pilot, he is perhaps second only to the legendary John Lankester Parker (Chief Test Pilot from 1918 to 1945) in his achievements for the company in this role. Brooke-Smith test-flew a large number of types from the Stirling and the Sunderland to the Sealand, Sperrin and the Canberra, the SB.1, SB.4, SB.5 and SC.1. The company magazine, *Short Story*, recorded that 'Brookie' would be sorely missed, "the familiar bellow over the telephone, the explosive comment that is always frank – take it or leave it – the sense of fun and the slight air of the buccaneer that Brookie takes with him wherever he goes. The masterly demonstrations of the SC.1 at Farnborough have been a great and fitting climax to a distinguished flying career." Brooke-Smith began flying in 1934 and made his first solo in a DH Gipsy Moth on his 17th birthday. All told by the time he retired as a test pilot he had flown 150 types of aeroplane from sailplanes to airliners and from helicopters to bombers. His major role in the development of the SC.1 had been marked in February 1959 by the award of the Derry and Richards Memorial Medal of the Guild of Air Pilots and Air Navigators (GAPAN). The following year he was the recipient of the Royal Aero Club's prestigious Britannia Trophy and the Royal Automobile Club's Segrave Trophy. In 1961 he was elected a Fellow of the Royal Aeronautical Society. From 1985 to 1986 he was the Master of GAPAN, following in the footsteps of John Lankester Parker. Brookie died in 1991 at the age of 73.

G-ARTZ in flight beside Strangford Lough.
(Herbie Edgar)

McCandless M-2 G-ARTZ. *(Herbie Edgar)*

The cockpit of G-ARTZ. *(Herbie Edgar)*

The irrepressibly inventive Rex McCandless (1915–1992) from Culcavy, Hillsborough, was, like Harry Ferguson and James Martin, a Co Down man. Largely self-taught and eccentric, he is remembered for a wide range of work, including motorcycles, four wheel drive cars, a cross country vehicle, plastics and a kiln for firing bricks. During the Second World War, Rex spent some time employed by Shorts, working, among other tasks, on the braking system of the Bristol Bombay. In 1960, he began to take an interest in gyroplanes,

specifically the American Bensen Aircraft Corporation's gyrocopter. Believing the design to be flawed in some respects he nevertheless used it as the basis of his first McCandless gyroplane, G-ARTZ, which he designed with the help of Frank Robertson and other engineers from Shorts. During the 1960s, he test-flew and developed five gyroplanes, including a two-seater, G-ATXY, using Triumph and Norton motorcycle and Volkswagen car engines. Meanwhile, a young Belfast mechanical engineer, WH 'Bill' Ekin had built a Bensen

Bill Ekin in flight. *(Bill Ekin)*

The final McCandless gyroplane, G-ATXX, at Ards on 11 February 1967. *(Ernie Cromie Collection)*

Rex McCandless in the ultimate variant of his gyroplane. *(Ernie Cromie Collection)*

McCandless autogyro at Ards. *(Ernie Cromie Collection)*

gyrocopter which he flew at Nutts Corner airfield, close to Crumlin Woollen Mill which became his base. Enthused, he purchased a gyroplane from Rex (G-ATXW) and secured the rights to build the McCandless machines. In 1969 and 1970, he formed two companies to build and market, respectively, McCandless-type gyroplanes. After many essential changes to the McCandless design and with the help of the retired Squadron Leader Desmond Mock as test pilot, the outcome was the WHE 'Airbuggy'. Despite many setbacks, including the collapse of the mill roof on top of two machines and several crashes, by the 1980s Bill had succeeded in building and selling six Airbuggys. The McCandless M-2, G-ARTZ and the M-4, G-ATXX are part of the collection at the Ulster Folk and Transport Museum, the first being held in storage, while the second is on display.

A model of the proposed HDM.106 posed as if in flight. *(via The Miles Aircraft Collection)*

Frank Robertson in June 1958. *(Bombardier Belfast)*

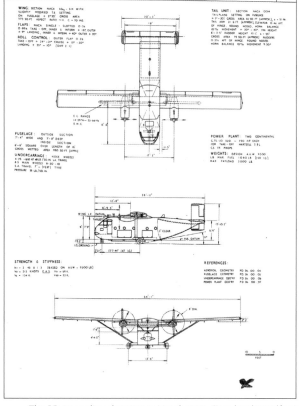

The PD.36 outline drawing in March 1961. *(Bombardier Belfast)*

In 1958 FG Miles Ltd approached Shorts with proposals for a collaborative venture developing and producing the Hurel-Dubois Miles 106 (HDM.106) Caravan light cargo aeroplane concept, which had itself been developed concurrently with the HDM.105 experimental project of 1955–58. The Caravan's origins were a blend of the Miles Aerovan of 1945 and a high aspect ratio wing (long and narrow) developed by Hurel-Dubois. Shorts decided not to manufacture the HDM.106. Hugh Conway noted that after a number of "differences of opinions" between the two companies, and also recognising Miles' precarious financial state said, "Enough is enough, we will buy it and make any further decisions an internal

matter". So Shorts purchased the preliminary design and all the test data gathered from the aircraft's trials. In part-payment for the deal, Miles was given the contract to design the flaps for the Belfast freighter. In April 1959, Shorts established a Light Aircraft Division under the leadership of Frank Robertson as Chief Designer. From this sequence of events evolved Preliminary Design 36 (PD.36), which was based on a considerable redesign and refinement of the original HDM design principal. The construction of two prototypes was authorised as a private venture (no UK Treasury support) and on a strictly limited budget.

Skyvan Astazou prototype G-ASCN takes off from Sydenham in October 1963. (Bombardier Belfast)

The Skyvan prototype nears completion in December 1962. (Bombardier Belfast)

SHORT SC.7 SKYVAN
Light Transport Aircraft

The cover of an early company brochure, showing the Skyvan powered by Continental piston engines. (Bombardier Belfast)

The most commercially successful range of aircraft designed and built by Shorts post-1945 was undoubtedly the series of light transports developed from the original PD.36, now re-designated as the SC.7 Skyvan. The prototype, G-ASCN, flew for the first time at 11.15 am on 17 January 1963, in the hands of Denis Tayler, the Chief Test Pilot. "After a flight lasting only a few minutes, the portly shape scurried – or should it be trundled? – home pursued by a menacing snow cloud." A cartoon in the same issue of *Short Story* depicted the aircraft as a removals van, complete with pilot clad in flat cap and overalls putting his feet up on an adjacent sofa. The Skyvan had a fixed undercarriage and was decidedly cuboid in shape. The sales brochure described it thus, "When Shorts set out to build the

The Short Skyvan prototype G-ASCN over Belfast Lough in December 1963. *(Bombardier Belfast)*

A Skyvan of the Royal Air Force of Oman lands in the desert. *(Bombardier Belfast)*

The cover of a Skyvan sales brochure. *(Bombardier Belfast)*

Skyvan they did not just make an aeroplane and see how much could be fitted into it. They started the other way round. First, they built a big flying box. They made it easy to get things into this box by making the back end of the box into a door. Shorts made it strong and rugged. It will go almost anywhere, land on the most primitive airstrips and it's very easy to maintain. But the surprising thing about the Skyvan is its limitless versatility. It takes only minutes to convert from a 19-passenger aircraft to a freighter carrying a load of 4600 lbs. It stands up to gruelling day and night operations without a murmur. Military uses include paratrooping, troop transport, supply dropping, vehicle ferry, counter-insurgency, clandestine warfare, casualty evacuation and civil disaster relief. Skyvan is not just a new aircraft. It's a new kind of aircraft. It's a bus, a train, a boat, a lorry, a car, a van – and it flies." Perhaps the most striking sales

A Skyvan Skyliner variant under production at Shorts. *(Bombardier Belfast)*

photograph was captioned, "An ox-cart off loads the flying box-cart at an equatorial jungle airstrip." The power units were changed from the 390 hp Continental piston engines of the prototype (Mk 1) to Astazou turboprops (Mk 1A and 2) and then to the much more satisfactory Garret TPE-331s (Mk 3, 3A, 3M and Skyliner). Never a glamorous aeroplane, the Skyvan was a best seller for Shorts until

surpassed by models developed from this basic but very practical concept. The first customer deliveries were made in 1966; to Aeralp in June and to Emerald Airways in August. Production ceased in 1986 after the 153rd example, which was delivered to the Amir Guard Air Wing, Sharjah.

Belfast with Sea King, Nimrod, Harrier and Chinook at Ascension Island. *(Bob Shackleton)*

A unique formation of all 10 Belfasts on 23 December 1971. *(Bombardier Belfast)*

Belfast XR364 over the docks in its home city in 1965. *(Bombardier Belfast)*

Another significant design was the mighty SC.5 Belfast freighter, the largest aircraft ever flown by the RAF (until the advent of the C-17 Globemaster III over 30 years later). On 5 January 1964, XR362 took off from Sydenham and, flown by Shorts' Chief Test Pilot Denis Tayler with co-pilot Peter Lowe and a crew of six, crossed Belfast Lough to perform its first landing at Aldergrove. In the event, Tayler's approach was too high and too fast and he had to overshoot. Three Belfasts flew together at the Farnborough Air Show in September, with XR364 disgorging 24 tons of Army vehicles on landing. On 23 December 1971 all ten Belfasts flew together in formation from 53 Squadron's base at RAF Brize Norton. XR362 later became

Samson of 53 Squadron and many years afterwards in 1977 was re-registered as G-BEPE, making the first revenue earning flight as a civil freighter for TAC Heavylift on 15 March 1980. In all, Heavylift Cargo Airlines bought five Belfasts, several of which were to prove of immense value during the Falklands Conflict in 1982, delivering vitally needed stores to Ascension Island, thereby making something of a mockery of the decision to remove these aircraft from the RAF's inventory in 1976. The very last Belfast to fly (formerly XR365 *Hector* and G-HLFT) has been parked at Cairns International Airport in Queensland since 2010. *Enceladus*, XR371, is preserved at the RAF Museum, Cosford. In 1954 Shorts had initiated a worldwide survey

Denis Tayler with the proposed jet-engined version of the Belfast. *(Bombardier Belfast)*

Chief Designer CD Hatton. *(Bombardier Belfast)*

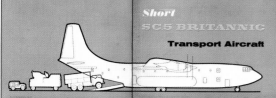

An early sales brochure before the Britannic was renamed Belfast. *(Bombardier Belfast)*

The prototype Belfast, G-ASKE (later XR362 and G-BEPE), being rolled out on 8 October 1963. *(Bombardier Belfast)*

of the likely requirements for air cargo aircraft. The company's expertise in the construction of large flying boats was now no longer commercially relevant, so seeking alternative large landplanes was a very reasonable idea. The study developed into the PD.15, which was to be powered by four piston engines and to have a twin-boom layout with large clamshell doors to the rear – not unalike the subsequent Armstrong Whitworth Argosy. The PD.16 followed which was similar in appearance but of much greater capacity with twin turboprop engines. Thereafter the project was redefined and christened the PD.18 Britannic. Originally it was planned to make substantial use of Britannia components, readily available from the

production line in Belfast. The early design team consisted of David Keith-Lucas, Hugh Conway and Frank Robertson. In 1958, CD Hatton was appointed Chief Designer of a large team. As the design progressed, every week it became less of a fat, high-wing Britannia and more a completely new aeroplane. By 1960 it had been renamed the Belfast. The load capacity of the aircraft was excellent both in weight and volumetric terms. Typical military loads were given in a company leaflet as, "Two Abbot self-propelled guns or three Saladin armoured cars or four Whirlwind helicopters or six Ferret scout-cars or two Jumbo cranes or ten Landrovers or two SRN-5 hovercraft or six Shorts armoured cars or 201 troops." It was hoped, however, that

A yacht being loaded into a Heavylift Belfast. *(Guy Warner Collection)*

The first Belfast and Skyvan together. *(Bombardier Belfast)*

A mock-up of the proposed civil passenger version of the Belfast. *(Bombardier Belfast)*

civil operators would be attracted by the capability offered, especially for outsize loads. Power was supplied by four Rolls-Royce Tyne turboprops, which gave the Belfast a cruising speed of 352 knots and a maximum range of 5300 miles. Developing the autoland capability (in partnership with Smiths) was a task of considerable complexity. It was the first military aircraft in service to incorporate the Smith Series Five Flight Control System, providing triplexed autoland capability, making it the largest aircraft in the world to make fully automatic landings. Further developments of the aircraft were planned – for tactical operations from rough strips, with uprated engines and larger propellers to increase performance, a swing-nose, double-deck

civil transport (carrying up to 249 passengers), a Skybolt missile platform or with a new wing and tail (adapted from the Lockheed C-141 Starlifter) and fitted with turbofan engines. As *Flight* magazine stated in 1963, "No company ever tried harder to perfect all aspects of a sound basic aeroplane than have Short & Harland with the Belfast. No company ever tried harder to develop it to meet every conceivable future requirement." But the orders never came and the support received from the government was less than ideal – the original contract was predicated on an order for 30 aircraft, which was then cut to only ten and nearly brought the company to ruin, as only a third of the non-recurring costs were now recoverable.

Roy Jenkins, the Minister of Aviation, flew from Queen's Island to Northolt in a Belfast in May 1965. *(Bombardier Belfast)*

Top centre: CE 'Denis' Wrangham. *(Bombardier Belfast)*

Many of the photos in this book would have been taken by Company Chief Photographer, Herbie Edgar, who worked for Shorts from 1946 to 1981. Here he prepares to record RN Seacat trials in 1965. *(Bombardier Belfast)*

Left: On 28 July 1965 Lord Plowden visited Shorts and is seen here with Denis Wrangham. *(Bombardier Belfast)*

By 1965 Shorts had a total payroll of some 7800 employees, of whom 6100 were employed on aircraft and related work, 1300 on precision engineering (including guided weapons) and the balance of 400 on general engineering. The annual turnover was in the region of £14 million. However, confidence in an aircraft manufacturing future for Belfast was not enhanced by the publication of the UK Government's Plowden Report at the end of 1965, which recommended the amalgamation of Britain's aircraft manufacturers into two large companies – a place for Shorts within this scheme was not envisaged. The Minister of Aviation, Roy Jenkins, who flew from Queen's Island to Northolt in a Belfast in May 1965, told Shorts, "You know that the Plowden Report isn't favourable towards you", which was something of an understatement. Nor was the company in any fit state to go it alone as a commercial manufacturer, since

it had existed for years on a diet of military contracts. A report from a consultancy firm stated, "It has no commercial marketing organisation worthy of the name and a management group which is experienced almost exclusively in supplying the requirements of one customer. Performance and adherence to a particular schedule of deliveries is generally paramount. Price is a secondary consideration. Extensive and continuous formal documentation of production progress, engineering changes and justification of any changes in the cost is required by the military. The net result is the need for a high proportion of indirect workers of all kinds – technical, managerial and administrative – to direct labour; which could not be justified in a normal commercial business". One of the unsung heroes of this period was undoubtedly the Chairman, CE 'Denis' Wrangham, who was tireless in his efforts on the Company's behalf.

VC-10 Sub-contract work in 1964.
(Bombardier Belfast)

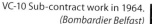

Tom Brooke-Smith flew this Royal Navy Hiller HT Mk 1 in 1954. *(Bombardier Belfast)*

Middle right: An artist's impression of the HS 681. *(BAe Systems)*

Right: The Breguet 941. *(Ateliers D'Aviation L Breguet)*

Further useful sub-contracting work came to Shorts in 1964 with forward and aft fuselage sections for the Vickers VC-10 airliner. It was anticipated that the Hawker Siddeley 681 STOL (short take-off and landing) military transport would also provide work for the company but in 1965 the RAF cancelled its order and it was never built. Proposals had also been made in the early 1960s with regard to collaborating with the French company, Breguet, on its 941/942 STOL transport, manufacturing Chance-Vought Crusader jet fighters with Rolls-Royce engines for the Royal Navy and Hiller 12E helicopters for the British Army but none of these plans came to fruition. Two Hiller Model 12E, G-ASIG and G-ASIH, were assembled at Queen's Island in May 1963 as a familiarisation exercise. Nor indeed did a plan in 1977 to buy the Britten-Norman Division of Fairey Aviation – the manufacturers of the Islander and the Trislander.

The Phantom outer wing production line.
(Bombardier Belfast)

The unusual overwing position of the VFW 614's engines may clearly
be seen in this photograph. *(Guy Warner Collection)*

Apprentices working on the Sea Hawk in 1982. *(Bombardier Belfast)*

The genesis of what was ultimately to become an extremely successful aerostructures division at Shorts was the undertaking made in 1965 to design and develop the wings for the new Fokker F.28 Fellowship short-range jet airliner. Another major sub-contract operation at this time was for the outer wings for the McDonnell Douglas Phantom. Engine pods were also built for the very unusual looking German VFW 614 short-haul airliner, which unfortunately was not a commercial success. Additional work was provided between 1962 and 1967 with the cocooning and storage of 239 obsolescent Fleet Air Arm aircraft: Sea Hawks, Sea Venoms, Gannets, Meteors, Hunters, Sea Devons and Sea Princes. One Sea Hawk FB5, WN108, was given to the Company's Apprentice School in 1964 for 'hands-on' training. In 1988, after some 2000 apprentices had passed through the School, Shorts decided that a more modern airframe was required and donated WN108 to the Ulster Aviation Society.

Philip Foreman on his appointment
as Managing Director in 1967.
(Bombardier Belfast)

An annotated photo of the
Company's main site in Belfast.
(Bombardier Belfast)

Only three years after becoming Chief Engineer in 1964, Philip Foreman was promoted once more, this time to Managing Director (he had been appointed to the Board of Directors in 1965 and had become Deputy Managing Director in the following year). Now the destiny and direction of one of the most important parts of Northern Ireland's industrial base was his responsibility, quite a remarkable rise after only nine years with the company. This was reported in the *Belfast Telegraph* on 3 January 1967, which quoted the newly appointed MD as follows, "There is no reason why the company should not develop another aircraft along the same lines as the Skyvan. But I can't see us doing anything as big as the Belfast freighter again. It's just too large an aeroplane for us." When asked about Shorts' future prospects he responded in typical style, "Certainly Shorts has a viable future. Do you think I would be here if

it didn't?" adding, "It will be a long, hard grind and a lot of hard work but we are going to get through." The problems which had to be faced were severe, "We had to make major decisions on where our future best lay, especially since the production of the Belfast was rapidly coming to an end. With a business based predominantly on the manufacture of military aircraft against Ministry of Defence orders, we clearly had to re-think our plans." One obvious option was to re-trench, cut back and concentrate on the growing and successful missiles business. Instead Philip Foreman's policy after becoming MD was to make the missile business one facet of a tripartite structure, the other two components being a small civil transport aeroplane and aerostructures, the building blocks already being in place for both of these.

RAF Tigercat deployed at Sydenham.
(Bombardier Belfast)

Seacat launch. (Bombardier Belfast)

Tigercat missiles ready to launch. (Thales Belfast)

As well as developments improving the basic naval Seacat, which included transistors replacing thermionic valves and the production of the lightweight, three-round launcher; a land-based system had been introduced. The Commandant of RAF Regiment, Air Chief Marshal Sir Philip Joubert de la Ferté had seen the need for an airfield defence system and had pressed for the development of what would become Tigercat, the first firing of which was in 1967. It was tested by the RAF Regiment in a deployment around Sydenham. It was cheap, adaptable and comparatively simple, with a launcher and control console capable of being towed by Land Rover. It was to sell well and entered service with No 48 Squadron RAF in September 1970. The Defence Sales Organisation, which was established by Denis Healey when he was Minister of Defence between 1964 and 1970, worked closely with Shorts, providing information from Defence Attaches around the world, on the lines of, "There's a ship being built – perhaps you can sell Seacat there." But this would not be enough to keep in employment most of those who depended upon the company for their livelihood.

Testing Blowpipe at Helen's Bay. *(Bombardier Belfast)*

A Blowpipe is readied for firing. *(Bombardier Belfast)*

A Blowpipe missile being fired. *(Thales Belfast)*

A new missile was being developed to add to the highly successful Seacat and Tigercat portfolio. Blowpipe was designed as a shoulder-launched, man-portable weapon. It was compact and responsive, taking only 20 seconds to warm-up and, not being a heat-seeker like Stinger it could take a target head-on. Some development work was carried out at Shorts' Guest House and farm at Helen's Bay. Dummy missiles were tested by being fired into a haystack. The first shoulder firing was in 1968 and in time it would win multi-million pound orders from the British Army, the Royal Marines and overseas customers. The principal of "engineering simplicity through design innovation" is well illustrated by the guidance and control system developed for Blowpipe – the rotating nose missile concept, which is simple but highly effective. Blowpipe was the first missile built by the company which was fully assembled in Northern Ireland. This required the establishment of a secure site where the explosive warhead could be handled safely. A former Admiralty torpedo testing depot near Crossgar was selected and was supplied with the explosives by air, firstly by Skyvan or SD3-30 from Glasgow to Aldergrove and from there by RAF helicopter to Crossgar.

The 600th RB211 pod is completed in November 1980. *(Bombardier Belfast)*

A RB211 nose cowl. *(Bombardier Belfast)*

The next stage in the development of the aerostructures side of Shorts' business was recalled by Sir Philip Foreman as follows, "By good fortune, at this time (May 1968) Rolls-Royce were launching the RB211 engine and were looking for suppliers to design and manufacture the engine nacelle so that they could market a complete powerplant instead of a bare engine. We managed to secure the contract for the nose cowl and for the final assembly of the complete nacelle around the engine. This work put us into a specialist niche where we could employ all our skills from aerodynamics through structures and systems to manufacture. By spotting and exploiting that market opportunity, we were able to become one of the world's leading manufacturers of nacelles for large turbofan engines." When a party of senior managers from Rolls-Royce visited Belfast to discuss the nacelles project they were not greatly impressed by the low level of activity in the aircraft factory but a visit to the nearby manufacturing facility for Seacat reassured them regarding Shorts' capability. This process was not without difficulty however as Rolls-Royce had over-extended itself with the RB211 programme and was obliged to declare bankruptcy in early 1971. Some 20% of Shorts' annual turnover was derived from engine podding, so the potential implications were severe. Fortunately both Rolls-Royce and Shorts were to survive this crisis and prosper. Blowpipe and Seacat orders kept the company afloat while the Government bailed out Rolls-Royce. From this beginning, Shorts became the leading European specialist in engine nacelle design, development and production.

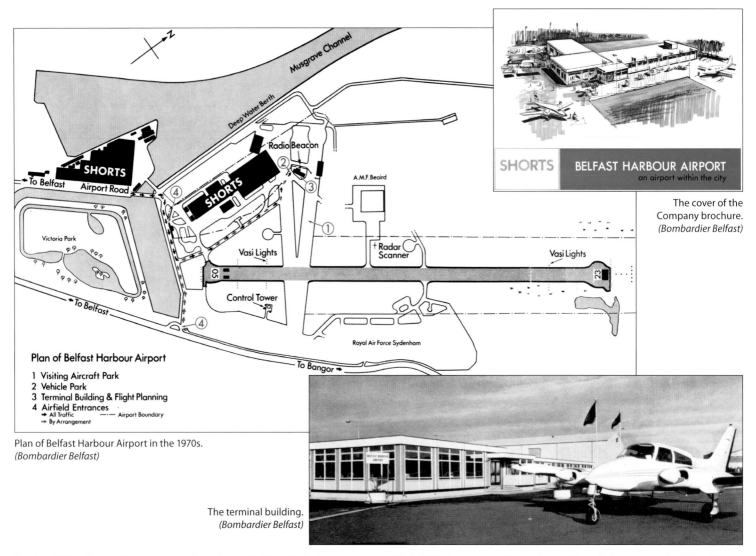

The cover of the
Company brochure.
(Bombardier Belfast)

Plan of Belfast Harbour Airport in the 1970s.
(Bombardier Belfast)

The terminal building.
(Bombardier Belfast)

In the 1970s Shorts began to market the airfield at Sydenham as Belfast Harbour Airport, using the slogan "an airport within the city". The aim at this stage was not to attract scheduled airline services but rather to encourage air taxi companies and chartered freight operators. An example of the latter, given in the company brochure, was Saturn Airways, "whose Hercules aircraft fly giant podded RB211 engines direct from Shorts' factory to Lockheed's works in California." Now, some 40 years later, George Best Belfast City Airport is a testament to the Company management's vision. For a few years in the 1960s, the Company also acted as sales agent for Beechcraft light aircraft in the British Isles until 1966 and indeed also proposed adaptations of Beech designs for the RAF.

An RB211 is loaded into Pacific Western C-130 CF-PWX at Sydenham on 4 December 1972. *(Bombardier Belfast)*

A modern operations room was among the facilities available. *(Bombardier Belfast)*

Beechcraft aircraft on view at Shorts.
(Bombardier Belfast)

Passengers leave an air taxi for a short car journey to the city centre.
(Bombardier Belfast)

The first two SD3-30s fly in formation. *(Bombardier Belfast)*

SD3-30 of Command Airways in flight over Sydenham. *(Bombardier Belfast)*

A 3-30 for Golden West Airlines. *(Bombardier Belfast)*

Two highly successful in-house designs were derived from the Skyvan, the first of which was the 30 seat SD3-30. The first flight was made by G-BSBH on 22 August 1974. Eight days earlier the initial order for three aircraft had been placed by Command Airways of Poughkeepsie, New York. The company's sales brochure described the aircraft's attributes, "This 30-seat, luxurious, highly economic aircraft introduces completely new standards to the world's commuter passengers and airlines. It is the first wide-body design developed specifically for short-haul operation and incorporates a range of passenger-appeal features unique in its class – walk-about headroom, air-conditioning, large windows, luxury seating, overhead lockers, galley and toilet facilities and in-flight cabin service. Complementing its big jet comfort, the 3-30's PT6A-45R turboprop engines, driving five-bladed propellers, make it one of the world's quietest airliners. It is the logical growth vehicle to replace Metro, Twin Otter, Beech 99 and similar aircraft on developing networks". It was aimed specifically at short-range regional and commuter traffic in the USA, following a decision by the US Civil Aeronautics Board to permit commuter and air taxi operators to use aircraft carrying up to 30 passengers. This was something of a

A design which did not progress beyond the concept stage, the Shorts 335. *(Bombardier Belfast)*

David Kennedy of Aer Lingus and Sir Philip Foreman at the official hand-over of a 330 to the airline on April 11, 1983. *(Bombardier Belfast)*

Short 330 G-BDBS, the pre-production prototype, now part of the Ulster Aviation Society's collection. *(Bombardier Belfast)*

triumph for Shorts, a relatively small UK-based company influencing the decision makers in Washington. Sales in the USA were helped by the 'Deregulation' policy of 1978 which served to stimulate wide demand for increased commuter services by removing government control from commercial aviation and exposing the passenger airline industry to market forces. One hundred and seventy-nine were produced, the first commercial service being flown by Time Air of Alberta, Canada on 24 August 1976. The final aircraft to be constructed were the last of 16 enhanced performance Sherpa C-23B light freighters for the US Army Air National Guard in August 1992.

At the handover of the final aircraft the Vice-President Operations, Ken Brundle said, "This line of historic aircraft covers thirty years of development, production and support, during which time 460 aircraft were delivered worldwide, with the vast majority still in extensive use today." A maritime patrol version, the SD3-MR Seeker, was proposed but did not enter production. Two other passenger variants, the 33-seat 333 and the 35-seat 335, were designed but were never officially announced and progressed no further than the drawing board. G-BDBS, the second pre-production prototype 330, is now resident at Maze/Long Kesh as part of the Ulster Aviation Collection.

A C-23 Sherpa cargo aircraft crewman Company E, 207th Aviation Battalion displays the unit patch on his flight suit. *(US Army)*

A C-23 over the German countryside. *(USAF)*

A C-23 on the ramp at Balad AB, Iraq in 2006. *(US Army)*

Previously, 18 C-23A Sherpas had been supplied to the 10th Military Airlift Squadron of the US Air Force and had given excellent service as part of the European Distribution System of spares support for combat aircraft, winning numerous awards and with the Company consistently being graded as outstanding with Contractor Logistics Support. The C-23A made its maiden flight on 6 August 1984. The first two aircraft were handed over to the USAF in November 1984 just eight months after the announcement of the contract award. The Sherpa was fitted with a full length rear ramp door which permitted the handling of the variety of loads required, ranging from LD3 containers up to the TF30 engine with afterburner.

Twenty-eight more C-23B+ aircraft were supplied to the US Army Air National Guard (ANG) – converted from ex-civil Short 360s. In recent years these aircraft have given very valuable service in Iraq, being able to operate from rudimentary airstrips, "carrying the same load as a Chinook but at a fraction of the cost". The ANG first deployed Sherpas to Kuwait in August 2003. The C-23s moved to Joint Base Balad, Iraq in 2004, serving airstrips from Mosul in the north to Kuwait in the south, logging, for example, in the case of the Alaska ANG, more than 1400 flight hours, and transporting 1800 personnel and 1.5 million pounds of cargo in a span of four months of its year-long deployment, using the skills the aircrews

Making ready to parachute from a C-23. *(US ANG)*

Flying the C-23. *(US ANG)*

A C-23 and C-5 Galaxy somewhere in Germany. *(USAF)*

had learned as bush pilots in the challenging flying conditions of the far north. "The Sherpa is the aircraft that can," said Lieutenant Colonel Steven Campfield, commander of the 6th Battalion, 52nd Aviation Regiment, which included the Sherpa company from the Georgia ANG, "I would say the Sherpa has been the workhorse in this theater." Over the next eight years the C-23s specialised in the delivery of time-critical supplies such as blood, food, water, spares, ammunition and key personnel, including special operations troops, flying at ultra low-level to avoid anti-aircraft fire (often less than 100 feet at 200 mph) and accumulating in excess of 47,000 flying

hours. At home and further afield they also assisted with disaster relief; including Hurricane Mitch in 1999, Hurricane Katrina in 2005, the earthquake in Haiti in 2010, searching for oil slicks in the Gulf of Mexico after the Macondo oil well blowout of 2010 and the aftermath of superstorm Sandy in 2012. As recently as May 2013, an Oklahoma-based Sherpa flew food to troops responding to the mega-tornado that struck the town of Moore. They also have helped fight wildfires in many of the Western states, were used during the 2010 Winter Olympics in Vancouver and regularly provided airlift for Special Operations forces during parachute training,

The flight crew, from the left, John Bailie, Chief Test Pilot Lindsay Cumming and Peter Rankin, pose after the first flight of G-ROOM on 1 June 1981. *(Bombardier Belfast)*

The 360 prototype, G-ROOM, flies over Sydenham, Queen's Island and Victoria Park. *(Bombardier Belfast)*

The second major derivative, the Short 360 (or Shed as it was affectionately known by its pilots) had a lengthened fuselage which could accommodate 36 passengers and a single tailfin rather than the twin fins of the Skyvan and 330. It also incorporated a three foot fuselage plug ahead of the wing and uprated PT6A-65R engines. These major changes assisted in reducing drag, a higher cruising speed and permitted an increased payload. The bottom line for the airline – seat mile costs – was reduced by 15%, with the result that the aircraft could make money at load factors below 40%. Toilet and galley facilities were improved and the baggage volume was significantly greater. The overall design philosophy was, "We will only change those systems and components which are directly affected by the airframe stretch, the engines or the tail unit or which from 330 experience have unacceptably high ownership costs arising from high replacement or overhaul costs." The launching of the aircraft was revealed at press conferences in London and Washington DC on 10 July 1980. The unique 'simultaneous' gatherings were made possible due to the five hour time difference which allowed Philip Foreman and the Executive Director Aircraft, Alex Roberts, to fly between the two capital cities by British Airways Concorde. The

Aer Lingus Short 360 EI-BSP. *(Bombardier Belfast)*

Three Short 360s are handed over to Michael Bishop of the Airlines of Britain Group in March 1984. *(Bombardier Belfast)*

The 360 production line at Shorts. *(Bombardier Belfast)*

prototype, G-ROOM first flew on 1 June 1981. The 360 entered passenger service with Suburban Airlines of Reading, Pennsylvania on 1 December 1982 serving a 700 miles, eight-city commuter route network. In 1985 the 360 Advanced with uprated and more fuel-efficient engines entered production. The final 360 variant was the 300 Series of 1987, which incorporated a number of refinements, including six-bladed Hartzell propellers, which significantly reduced noise. Production ceased in 1991 with the last of the line being delivered to Rheinland Air Services after 164 examples. A survey of regional aircraft in 1993 gave the 360 this testimonial, "For regional airlines requiring a tough, unpressurised, 36-seater with a modest range, the Short 360 is probably an ideal choice." The 360 proved to be a reliable and popular design which gave airlines the ability to develop routes with much less financial risk than would have been the case with more sophisticated and expensive aircraft. The break-even load factor was as low as 39% (14 seats filled). The trouble free systems and easy maintenance permitted rapid turn-arounds and a dispatch reliability figure which routinely recorded 99%. It was also well-liked by the pilots who flew the aircraft, winning the ultimate accolade, "A real pilot's aeroplane".

Summit Air Skyvan, C-GJGS, at Isachsen Island in Nunavut, Canada in 2007. *(Paolo Dal Bello)*

Austrian Air Force Skyvans. *(Peter Dachgruber)*

Skyvans G-BEOL and G-PIGY of Invicta Aviation. *(Invicta Aviation)*

In 1984 there were well over 100 Skyvans operating worldwide with 46 operators in 32 countries in a remarkable variety of roles – maritime patrol in Singapore and Japan; passenger services in Norway, Malaysia, Greece and the Maldives; oil drilling support operations in Indonesia, South America and the Middle East; highway patrol in Thailand; mail deliveries in Venezuela; paratroop training in Austria; police duties in Lesotho and Malawi; aerial prospecting in Canada; welfare work in Mexico; mid-air retrieval of rocket-borne experiments in the USA; support duties for defence forces in Oman, Nepal, Botswana, Argentina, Guyana and Panama – plus a miscellany of other roles – which has continued into the 21st Century.

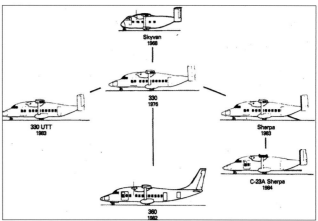

The Skyvan Family Tree.
(Bombardier Belfast)

A 360 and a 330
in formation.
(Bombardier Belfast)

An artist's impression of what was to be the
ultimate member of the family – the Shorts 450.
(Bombardier Belfast)

The basic square fuselage section of the Skyvan was retained for the two types developed from it, as was the method of fabrication, using a bonded metal structure and also the braced, high aspect ratio wing. This evolutionary family approach enabled Shorts to make full use of its investment in jigs, tools and fixtures, as well as minimising the inventory required through the use of common parts. Most importantly from the fiscal point of view, it enabled the variants to be launched without the enormous front end funding required by brand new designs and the technical risks associated with beyond state-of-the-art technology. These benefits were passed on to the customer in the form of lower first cost of the aircraft, which in turn was reflected by lower fare levels to the passenger, with consequent market stimulation and increased sales. It can be argued with a considerable degree of justification that the Shorts family of commuter aircraft transformed short range air travel and allowed many hitherto economically unviable routes to be exploited and developed. The final version of the family would have been the 45–49 seat Shorts 450. It is instructive to consider the following statistics: British Civil Aircraft Total Sales Figures in respect of the best selling aircraft since the Second World War – the Vickers Viscount 444, the BAe 146/Avro RJ 394, the Avro/HS/BAe 748 382, the BAC 1-11 244 but the Skyvan/330/360 family 496!

A Lear Fan in flight.
(Guy Warner Collection)

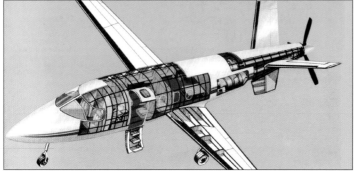

A cutaway drawing of the Lear Fan. (Guy Warner Collection)

The exterior of the composites factory in Newtownabbey. (Bombardier Belfast)

Following the closure of No 23 Maintenance Unit at RAF Aldergrove in 1978, the Government sought alternative industrial opportunities to utilise the skills and facilities available and to provide a palliative to the effects of 'The Troubles' on the Northern Ireland economy. To this end Lear Fan Ltd was formed in 1980 with the support of Northern Ireland Department of Economic Development. The Lear Fan 2100 project was ultimately a failure but it was a worthy effort. The aircraft was the final brainchild of William Powell (Bill) Lear, of Learjet fame. It was a revolutionary concept, a fuel efficient, high-speed, pusher propeller, eight-seat executive aircraft, made almost entirely from carbon composite material. Over 1000 jobs in Northern Ireland were projected by 1984, with the production flight testing being based at Aldergrove. By the end of 1980 125 people were employed at the factory in Newtownabbey, Co Antrim, rising to 470 a year later, peaking at 560 in 1982 and reducing by 90% in 1984 as financial difficulties mounted. It was intended that from the 43rd aircraft onwards the Lear Fan would have been fabricated and assembled in Northern Ireland entirely, and flown 'green' to the USA for fitting out with custom-built interiors. The prototype first flew from Reno, Nevada on 1 January 1981. Delays in the certification of the prototype in the USA, due to technical difficulties, caused financial problems, which proved insurmountable. The plan collapsed before any local assembly or flying was achieved, with the Company filing for bankruptcy in May 1985. All was not lost, as the factory and machinery in Newtownabbey was taken over by Shorts a few years later and formed the basis of its development as a world leader in the manufacture of advanced aerospace composite structures.

British Airways Lockheed Tristar. *(Bombardier Belfast)*

Aerostructure production clockwise from top left: The 500th engine pod for the BAe 146; main landing gear doors for the Boeing 747; a Fokker 100 wing in production; nacelles in production at Shorts. *(Bombardier Belfast)*

The aerostructures business continued to prosper. A good relationship had been established with Lockheed as the RB211 powered that company's L-1011 Tristar airliner, the wings for which were made by Avco in Nashville. One morning, Charlie Ames, the CEO in Nashville telephoned his opposite number in Belfast and asked if Shorts would like some work making components for the Tristar – ailerons, spoilers, wing tips, undercarriage doors. He added that he never made a deal without shaking hands on it. Philip Foreman was on a flight to Nashville the next day. A contract worth £20 million was agreed with British Aerospace in 1979 to manufacture engine pods for the BAe 146 regional airliner. Another very valuable contract was made with Boeing to supply wing components for the 757, adding to work already undertaken building main undercarriage doors for the Boeing 747. Later work for Boeing would include all composite rudder assemblies for the 737-300. By 1983 Shorts had delivered 1100 engine nacelle units and had risen to the second largest manufacturer in the world of these, 203 Fokker F.28 wings, 252 flight component sets for the Tristar, 345 sets of undercarriage doors for the 747 and the first 33 sets of inner flaps for the 757, with an annual turnover of £44 million. Later a risk-sharing partnership was agreed with Fokker on the successor to the F.28 Fellowship airliner. Shorts were to design, develop and build the advanced technology wings for the Fokker 100 – which included carbon-fibre components and which made its maiden flight from Amsterdam Schipol on 30 November 1986 – the wings having been transported to Holland in the HeavyLift Cargo Airlines Belfast G-HLFT, the first of many such trips. This was a very successful partnership until, in the mid-1990s, Fokker ran into financial difficulties and ceased operations shortly afterwards. In all, Shorts built the wings for 241 F.28s, 283 Fokker 100s and 48 Fokker 70s. Fokker in turn produced the outer wings for the Shorts 330 and 360.

Autoclaves No 1 and 2 at Newtownabbey. *(Bombardier Belfast)*

The 110 ton autoclave, the largest in Europe in 1981. *(Bombardier Belfast)*

Tex Boullioun opens the Metal Bonding and Composite Manufacturing Facility in June 1981. *(Bombardier Belfast)*

As part of its aerostructures business Shorts gained an enviable reputation in the field of the manufacture of composites. Philip Foreman had visited Boeing in Seattle, had been impressed by the work undertaken there and had come to the opinion that this was suitable work for Shorts, which already had manufactured some glass fibre and polyester resin items as far back as the 1950s. He was convinced by what he had seen that carbon fibre was the way ahead and that rivets were old hat. The first step was to make composite components for the Skyvan to gain experience. A 'clean room' was set up and a senior executive from Boeing, Wally Buckley, was invited over to Belfast to inspect it. As he ran his finger along a dusty ledge and asked, "Is this really a clean room?", it was one of the worst moments of the MD's time at Shorts – he felt about two feet

high. However he took the criticism on the chin, listened carefully to Boeing's advice and in 1981 a 110-ton autoclave was installed. When EH 'Tex' Boullioun, the President of the Boeing Commercial Airplane Company opened the facility on 11 June, Philip Foreman took great pleasure in hearing him pronounce himself highly impressed with what Shorts had achieved. The autoclave, which was the largest of its kind in Europe at that time, was used for the adhesive bonding of metal and carbon fibre aircraft components. The company went on from strength to strength and became one of the leaders in this field of manufacture. A manufacturing centre for components was opened in Dunmurry in the old DeLorean factory. Shorts also invested in high technology equipment – computer design systems and direct electronic links with Boeing in Seattle.

Sikorsky Black Hawk. *(Bombardier Belfast)*

Shorts and Sikorsky Offer Black Hawk to RAF

Mr William F Paul, President of Sikorsky Aircraft and Sir Philip Foreman in front of the Black Hawk after signing the collaborative agreement. *(Bombardier Belfast)*

A Piper PA-38 Tomahawk. *(Piper Aircraft Inc)*

A programme which looked to be very promising when it was announced in 1984 was the signing of a Memorandum of Agreement between Shorts and United Technologies' Sikorsky Aircraft to submit the Sikorsky S.70A Black Hawk as a candidate to meet the MOD's Air Staff Target 404 for 75 to 125 medium-lift support helicopters to replace the RAF's Wessex and Puma fleets. Shorts would have handled the production of major components and composite parts, final assembly, flight test, delivery, modifications and post-design services. Sir Philip commented at the time, "It will

proportion of military work. Additionally the technology exchange agreement under the terms of the MOA is especially significant and offers Shorts the possibility of entering entirely new fields of manufacturing technology." Sadly it was not to be, the RAF never received a helicopter under AST 404, the Wessex soldiered on until 2002 and the Puma is in service to this day, a number having been converted recently to Mk2 standard. An earlier agreement made at the end of the 1970s with the Piper Aircraft Corporation in the USA, to build the Piper Tomahawk light aircraft did not come to fruition

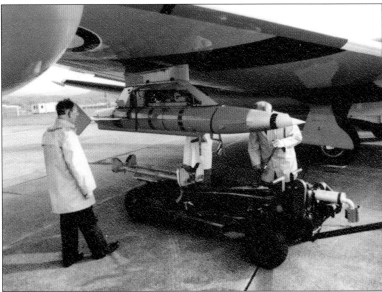

A Stiletto being mounted under the wing of a Canberra. (Bombardier Belfast)

Skeet military aircraft target. (Bombardier Belfast)

The armoured car production line in 1987. (Bombardier Belfast)

Shorland Armoured Patrol Car. (Bombardier Belfast)

To complete the picture, the Company was also involved in flying services activities, including the provision of maintenance and operational services for military and civil organisations. Aircraft target drones were maintained and operated for the Ministry of Defence in the UK and at the Woomera range in Australia. The company also produced: the Stiletto high altitude drone, capable of exceeding Mach 4, which was a variant of the Beech AQM-37A substantially re-engineered to meet British requirements and the MATS-B and Skeet military targets for the British Army, which were designed and manufactured by the Missile Systems Division to provide a low-cost, highly manoeuvrable drone for use in practice firings of close-range missiles and guns. Shorts also designed and manufactured the Shorland range of robust, low-cost, armoured internal security vehicles – patrol cars, personnel carriers, anti-hijack vehicles and other specialised units, all based on a strengthened version of the 109 inch Land Rover chassis. In production over three decades, the Shorlands established themselves as the best selling vehicles of their kind on the international market, seeing service in more than 40 countries.

The radio controlled Javelin system deployed and ready for action. *(Thales Belfast)*

Javelin Lightweight Multiple Launcher. *(Bombardier Belfast)*

Starburst was first unveiled during Operation Desert Storm in 1991. *(Thales Belfast)*

On the missiles side, Blowpipe was developed into the more advanced and easier to use Javelin, which was line of sight, radio controlled and with a semi-automatic guidance system. Another key change was the migration from the multi purpose blast and armour penetrating shaped charge warhead to a new warhead specific to air targets, with penetrating fragments made from tungsten. From 1984 onwards it was sold to a dozen armed forces in seven countries. Javelin was evolved in a highly secretive programme into a Laser Beam Riding missile called Javelin S15; incorporating a new guidance technology immune to all countermeasures, and developed by Shorts engineers in Belfast. This Laser Beam Riding system was under development for the new Starstreak missile but was rushed into service in the Starburst Missile for the first Gulf War in 1991. Javelin S15 was eventually sold successfully to many nations overseas as the Starburst Missile; in the Middle East, Far East and North America.

A Starstreak missile being fired from an Alvis Stormer. *(Thales Belfast)*

Starsteak multiple and single launchers. *(Bombardier Belfast)*

The Starstreak missile began development by Shorts in the early 1980s as a concept demonstrator. This included using the existing Javelin rocket motor with a smaller guidance kit mounted on the front to demonstrate a unique single actuator guidance concept to be used in the Starstreak programme. These demonstrators eventually led to the award in December 1986 of a £225 million contract from the Ministry of Defence for the development, initial production and supply of the Mach 3.5 (2660 mph) Starstreak, mounted on the Alvis Stormer vehicle, together with the lightweight multiple launcher and shoulder-launched variants, all for the British Army. Sir Philip Foreman commented, in a conversation with Eric Waugh, on these advanced missiles, "The new Starstreak factory at Castlereagh was the last capital expenditure I authorised before I retired. It was... is... a superb factory and inside it the equipment and the sort of work they are doing is unbelievable. They are working to tolerances which we thought were impossible – to tenths of a thousandth of an inch on a mass production basis."

An artist's impression of the Boeing 7J7. *(Boeing Commercial Airplane Company)*

Above: IAE V2500 engine nose cowl. *(Bombardier Belfast)*

V2500 engines power this Turkish Airlines A321. *(Guy Warner)*

The Company Chairman, Sir Philip Foreman, in 1983. *(Bombardier Belfast)*

In 1985, working in partnership with the US company, Rohr Industries of San Diego, a contract was won for the nacelles and other important components of the V2500 engine for the Airbus A-320. Sir Philip Foreman was interested in buying Rohr but the government would not consider the idea. A Memorandum of Understanding was signed with Boeing in March 1986 which provided for Shorts becoming a Programme Associate on the advanced technology Boeing 7J7 150 seat, twin prop-fan airliner. It was anticipated that this would bring a considerable volume of work to Belfast and was evidence of the esteem in which Shorts was held by Boeing. Sadly the project did not come to fruition and the 7J7 never took to the air.

A Kuwaiti Air Force Tucano. *(Bombardier Belfast)*

A Tucano takes off from Sydenham. *(Bombardier Belfast)*

A Tucano of 72(R) Squadron RAF in a special 90th anniversary colour scheme in 2008, flown by Flight Lieutenant Bobby Moore and AVO Erik Mannings. *(Geoffrey Lee, Planefocus Ltd)*

A Tucano and its predecessor, the Jet Provost, in formation. *(Bombardier Belfast)*

The last type wholly built in Belfast was an adaptation of the Embraer design from Brazil, the EMB-312 Tucano. The first flight was on 30 December 1986 and the first production model was ZF135 for the RAF. The Tucano was manufactured under licence with 130 being delivered to the RAF, 12 to the Kenya Air Force and 16 to the Kuwait Air Force. It was much modified from the Embraer original, with a 1150 shp Garrett TPE-331-12B engine driving a four-bladed Hartzell, fully feathering and reversing propeller, which gave higher performance in terms of speed and climb rate, a stronger airframe with increased fatigue life, ventral airbrake and restyled wingtips, the fitting of Martin–Baker MB 8LC ejection seats for both crew, bird-strike proofing of the cockpit canopy to UK standards and a complete systems/radio change to ensure maximum compatibility with the BAe Hawk, to which the student pilots would proceed. The Shorts- and Embraer-built Tucanos possessed only 50% commonality. The export T Mk 51s and 52s for Kenya and

Allan Deacon.
(Bombardier Belfast)

Tucano Zap. *(Bombardier Belfast)*

Tucanos under construction in Belfast. *(Bombardier Belfast)*

Kuwait featured enhanced avionics, upgraded air conditioning and provision for external ordnance on four wing stations, capable of mounting various rocket pods, cannons, bombs, and auxiliary fuel tanks. Tragedy struck the programme on 22 February 1990, when Allan Deacon, the Chief Test Pilot since 1984, was killed when the first Mk 51 Tucano, which he was flying, crashed into the sea in the North Channel due to flutter during high speed weapons carriage trials. The last complete aircraft manufactured at Sydenham was ZF516, c/n T131, which was delivered to the RAF on 25 January 1993. Aircraft E27 for Kuwait was finished in July 1991 but because of the Gulf War was not delivered until 1995. The Embraer-built Tucano, flown at Shorts as a development aircraft and registered G-BTUC, now forms part of the Ulster Aviation Collection at Maze/Long Kesh.

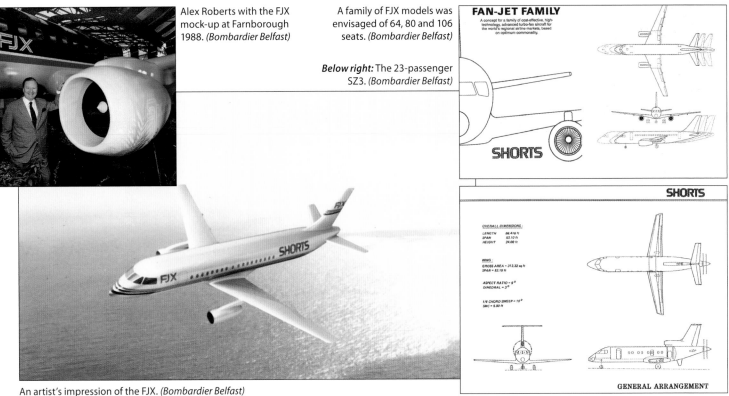

Alex Roberts with the FJX mock-up at Farnborough 1988. *(Bombardier Belfast)*

A family of FJX models was envisaged of 64, 80 and 106 seats. *(Bombardier Belfast)*

FAN-JET FAMILY

A concept for a family of cost-effective, high-technology, advanced turbo-fan aircraft for the world's regional airline markets, based on optimum commonality.

SHORTS

Below right: The 23-passenger SZ3. *(Bombardier Belfast)*

SHORTS

OVERALL DIMENSIONS :
LENGTH   66.416 ft
SPAN   53.10 ft
HEIGHT   24.09 ft

WING :
GROSS AREA = 313.32 sq ft
SPAN = 53.10 ft

ASPECT RATIO = 9°
DIHEDRAL = 3°

1/4 CHORD SWEEP = 10°
SMC = 5.90 ft

GENERAL ARRANGEMENT

An artist's impression of the FJX. *(Bombardier Belfast)*

As further development opportunities for the 330/360 family of aircraft came to a close and a production replacement became increasingly necessary, a series of potential collaborative programmes were investigated with likely partners, who were active or interested in regional aircraft projects. In particular, in 1986/7 detailed project studies were carried out with De Havilland Canada (then owned by Boeing) to identify a new design for the 20–30 seat market. Two turboprop project designs were produced, a fairly conventional aircraft and a more advanced 'pusher' concept, with twin-engines mounted in the tail – not dissimilar to the Lear Fan. It was believed that this radical idea would allow for enhanced aerodynamic and propulsive efficiency. However, due in part to management and economic problems at De Havilland, Boeing stopped all development work to concentrate on immediate production problems. By this time Shorts had become rather more interested in the possibilities

for a small regional jet in the 40–50 seat class. In the light of the advent of a new range of efficient turbofan engines, the project was rapidly developed and was revealed, complete with a full-scale mock-up of the cabin section, at the Farnborough Air Show in 1988. This was the FJX. The Sales and Marketing Director, Alex Roberts, commented, "The fuselage diameter now gives shoulder and aisle width identical to the MD-80 series and is substantially larger than the proposed Canadair Challenger 601RJ." It was a very attractive looking aeroplane not unlike a small Airbus in shape. The aim was to make a firm launch decision early in 1989. Presentations were made to over 60 airlines worldwide, considerable interest being shown and a detailed technical summary/development and production cost plan was written. Meanwhile, in Canada, Bombardier/Canadair were working on the aircraft mentioned by Alex Roberts.

Sir Philip was succeeded as Chief Executive and Chairman of Short Brothers plc by Roy McNulty CBE (later Sir Roy). *(Bombardier Belfast)*

Sir Philip with Mrs Thatcher. *(Bombardier Belfast)*

Sir Philip Foreman at the controls of the Ulster Aviation Society's SD3-30, G-BDBS. *(Ulster Aviation Society)*

In 1988 Sir Philip Foreman retired from his positions of Company Chairman, which he had held since 1983, and Managing Director, after holding this post for 21 years. His influence on Shorts over a period of 30 years was immense and he has with considerable justification been referred to in print as, 'the fourth Shorts brother.' He was the first to acknowledge the support of others, who included Tom Carroll, Chief Engineer Aircraft; Tom Johnston, Chief Aerodynamicist Aircraft; Malcolm Wild, Head of Projects Aircraft; Denis Tayler, Chief Test Pilot; Brian Carlin and Ken Brundle (successively the MD's Personal Assistant); Bob Manvell, General Manager Guided Weapons; Dick Ransom, Chief Project Designer Guided Weapons; Frank Maguiness, Chief Draughtsman Weapons. On the composites side there was George Crawford, who later rose to the position of Vice-President and presiding over finance from 1978, Roy McNulty. Philip Foreman was awarded the CBE in 1972 for services to industry and export and was knighted in 1981. In 1974 he was awarded the British Empire Gold Medal by the Royal Aeronautical Society. From 2003 he was the Patron of the Ulster Aviation Society and, along with his wife, Margaret, took a great and generous interest in the work of the Society. Sir Philip passed away just before his 90th birthday in 2013. He was a highly talented engineer and manager, who should to be remembered for his contributions to the British aerospace industry in general and to the industrial life of Northern Ireland in particular.

The interior fitting of a Bombardier business jet. *(Bombardier Belfast)*

A CRJ on the ground at Sydenham, provides an opportunity for Bombardier Shorts workers and families to look over the aircraft. *(Guy Warner)*

The CRJ 200 in flight. *(Bombardier Belfast)*

Shorts as a manufacturing company received a new lease of life and an injection of fresh ideas and capital in 1989, when it became part of the Canadian Bombardier Inc group. However, whilst bringing great benefits to the company, it spelt the end of the FJX. The Canadair RJ was selected for development as, being a derivative of the Challenger business jet, it represented a lower technical risk with reduced development and certification costs. Shorts were recompensed with significant design and production work on the initial version of the RJ. From this beginning, Shorts have continued as an important member of the Bombardier Group, which also includes the former Canadair, De Havilland Canada and Learjet companies, which were all acquired between 1986 and 1992.

The triple warheads on the Starstreak missile may be clearly seen in this image. *(Thales Belfast)*

The Starstreak Lightweight Multiple Launcher in action. *(Thales Belfast)*

A Starstreak Lightweight Multiple Launcher in position to protect the London 2012 Olympic Games. *(Thales Belfast)*

Turning again to missiles, Starstreak consists of a two stage rocket motor assembly with a payload consisting of three high density laser-guided 'darts'. The first stage motor accelerates the missile to approximately 200 mph in a fraction of a second. It is ejected from the tube and coasts for about 10 m at which point the main booster rocket motor ignites. This accelerates the missile to Mach 3.5 with a total time from trigger press to end of boost of about one second. During that time the missile also spins up to a high rate essential for the separation system to function. A piston assembly pushes the three darts forward at the end of boost breaking the retention system, and the darts are free to separate from the boost vehicle. The three individually guided darts each contain all the subsystems of a normal missile but in miniature form. The diameter of the Starstreak dart is about the same as a pound coin. Starstreak is still regarded as an exceptional weapon, and the pride of the engineers involved in the design is readily observable. It entered service in the mid 1990s and is expected to remain in service to at least 2025. Starstreak was a key element in the defensive system during the Olympic Games in London 2012, being positioned with the Lightweight Multiple Launcher on the roof of high rise buildings around the Olympic Park. Starstreak won accolades for its reliability and availability during that period.

Inside the Thales factory an ultra-clean environment is essential. *(Thales Belfast)*

The Thales factory at Castlereagh in Belfast. *(Thales Belfast)*

An artist's impression of FMRAAM. *(Thales Belfast)*

When Shorts was acquired by Bombardier in 1989 the missiles part of the business was named the Defence Systems Division. Bombardier began looking for a partner in the early 1990s. A relationship developed with Thomson-CSF whose radars, command and control systems and launchers were a good fit with the Castlereagh products. A 50:50 joint venture was signed in 1993 and Shorts Missile Systems Limited (SMS) was born. Unfortunately, however, between 1994 and 1996 the number of employees at Castlereagh declined from 1500 to 500, as part of the 'peace dividend' following the fall of the Iron Curtain. In 1999 Bombardier sold their 50% share in SMS to Thomson-CSF who re-branded and changed their name to Thales in 2000. In the late 1990s SMS had teamed with Raytheon Missile Systems from the USA in a competition to develop a beyond visual range air to air missile, BVRAAM. The Shorts/Raytheon bid, called FMRAAM (Future Medium Range Air to Air Missile), was based on an air breathing version of the successful AMRAAM (Advanced Medium Range Air to Air Missile). Shorts' involvement was to be in the wind tunnel testing of the missile, and aircraft stores separation testing, structural and environmental testing and also the final assembly, integrated test and check out of the missiles. Although the solution proposed by Shorts/Raytheon was lower risk and cost, the competition was won in 1999 by a European consortium headed up by the pan-European MBDA with Meteor.

Test firing a Hellfire missile from a British Army Apache at Yuma. *(Thales Belfast)*

A pair of Apaches at sunrise. *(Piers Lewis)*

Under the UK Apache Helicopter Industrial Participation Programme, Thales was awarded a contract in late 1997 from the Lockheed Martin Corporation in Orlando, Florida. The programme was manufactured under licence with Lockheed Martin (and Longbow Missiles partner Northrop Grumman) for an assembly and check-out of 2600 mix of Hellfire II and Longbow Missiles delivery to UK Ministry of Defence. A purpose built explosive assembly and test facility was constructed by mid-1999 at the Thales missile plant in Northern Ireland, the layout of which was based on the Lockheed Martin plant in Alabama, USA. Thales Assembly Operators were co-located and trained in Lockheed's Troy, Alabama Facility and actually assembled US Army missiles. Test Engineers were trained in Orlando. The excellent Lockheed/Thales Teamwork was a major success factor in the programme. Delivery to the UK customer commenced in late 2000 after First Article Test Qualification (at Redstone Arsenal Test Facility) and Flight Testing (at Eglin Air Force Base) and was completed in early 2003 on schedule with 100% performance on Batch Lot Quality Acceptance Testing. Thales was also contracted to produce 200 M299 Launchers for the UK Apache.

Thales participated in the VT1 missile replenishment programme for the French Air Force, Navy and other customers. *(Thales Belfast)*

A VT1 missile is launched. *(Thales Belfast)*

The VT1 missile and launcher. *(Thales Belfast)*

During 2000, the relationship with Thales provided a challenging opportunity for the Belfast business to participate in the VT1 missile replenishment programme for the French Air Force and Navy, as well as overseas customers. VT1 was the missile utilised by the Crotale NG Air Defence System. VT1 (Vought-Thomson 1) was originally developed in the late 1980s by a company called LTV (Ling-Temco-Vought) with critical subsystems from Thomson including the warhead, proximity sensor and receiver/transponder. LTV subsequently became Loral, which then became part of the Lockheed Martin group. The original 1000 missiles became obsolete in the early 2000s and Thales launched a 'Design, Development and Production Competition' for an updated VT1 missile to re-supply existing customers of the Crotale System. Thales Belfast won the

competition and launched the design phase in early 2001. The programme provided the opportunity to maintain and develop the key missile engineering skills required for Short Range Air Defence missiles. The missile was 76 kg with a maximum speed of Mach 3.5 and a range of out to 15 km. Although a much bigger missile than Belfast were used to (2.3 m for the VT1 compared to 1.3 m Starstreak), it required the same skills and experience in high supersonic missile design that had been developed in Belfast during the Starstreak programme. Although the missile had previously been in service, many features were obsolete and required complete redesign and obsolescence removal. The missile entered service in 2005, and more than 500 missiles have been built to date with further opportunities for missile sales being progressed today.

The Lightweight Multi-role Missile. *(Thales Belfast)*

An computer generated image of the LMM mounted on a Royal Navy Wildcat. *(Thales Belfast)*

The demand for Very Short Range Air Defence Systems fell off rapidly in the years after 2000. This was partly due to the reduced requirement for these types of weapons when air superiority was assured by the Allied Forces, such as in the Gulf Wars, and also partly due to reduced budgets within the Ministry of Defence. In 2006 some self-funded work commenced into studying the potential for a low cost multi-role munition for application on Land, Sea and Air Vehicles. Out of these studies came the concept for LMM (Lightweight Multi-role Missile) which was subsequently selected to provide a complimentary capability to Starstreak for the Ground Based Air Defence (GBAD) environment and also as the weapon of choice to meet the FASGW-Light (Future Anti-Surface Guided Weapon-Light) requirement for the Royal Navy Wildcat Helicopter. The LMM is a missile with a conventional configuration similar to that of the Starburst missile. However the nose section is roll stabilised providing a skid-to-turn guidance method rather than a twist and steer system used in both Starstreak and Starburst. The LMM missile is powered by a two stage rocket motor assembly which provided a maximum speed of around Mach 1.5. The missile was designed from the outset with modularity and re-use in mind and was fully compatible with the existing Starstreak ground equipment for shoulder launch, tripod launch and vehicle launch. The missile is currently in development and expected to enter service in 2015. LMM has positioned the company well with a robust airframe with modularity at its heart. Several variants have been proposed and demonstrated including seeker based versions. The economic climate for missile manufacturers in the UK remains extremely challenging, but LMM has the potential to provide much needed export opportunities in the future.

Irish Air Corps Lear 45 on the ramp at Nice Airport. *(Guy Warner)*

The design, manufacture and certification of the CRJ700's engine nacelles, including the thrust reversers is carried out in Belfast. *(Bombardier Belfast)*

The forward and centre fuselage for the Bombardier CRJ700 is designed and manufactured in Belfast. *(Bombardier Belfast)*

The work undertaken in recent years by Bombardier Aerospace in Belfast includes design and manufacturing as follows: the complete fuselage of the Learjet 45 and Learjet 75; the forward and mid-fuselage, engine nacelles and thrust reversers of the CRJ700 and CRJ900; forward and centre fuselage, tailplane, wing components and engine nacelles of the CRJ200; nacelles, flight control surfaces and main landing gear fairings of the Dash 8 Q400; 25% of the airframe – the forward fuselage, tail plane, engine nacelles and some composite structures for the Global Express; the mid-fuselage, horizontal stabiliser and engine nacelles of the Challenger 604 and the centre fuselage of the Continental Business Jet. The company is also a world leader in the field of advanced aerospace composites and retains its close association with Boeing as a supplier of aerostructures for a number of that company's civil aircraft programmes. Aircraft

The Challenger 604 business jet.
(Bombardier Belfast)

Since 2000, Belfast-born Michael J Ryan CBE, has been Vice President and General Manager of Bombardier Aerospace, Belfast.
(Bombardier Belfast)

Horizontal stabiliser for the Global Express.
(Bombardier Belfast)

A Global Express at Sydenham. *(Guy Warner)*

engine nacelle design, development and manufacture remains a highly important work area for contracts with Rolls-Royce, IAE and General Electric. Product support is provided to airlines which have Belfast-built nacelles, as well as to the owners of over 500 Shorts aircraft worldwide. Bombardier has brought many benefits to Belfast, but in return has gained from the "first assembly line manufacturers of aircraft in the world – building Wright biplanes in 1909 under licence from the brothers themselves" – programme management skills, worldwide marketing contacts and a solid aircraft engineering tradition. Bombardier Aerospace has become not only the world's leading manufacturer of business, regional and amphibious aircraft but also the third largest civil aircraft manufacturer. Its headquarters are in Montreal, Canada and it employs a global workforce in excess of 37,000.

A Short 360 of Alliance Air Charter. (*Alliance Air*)

A Short 360 of La Costeña in Nicaragua. (*La Costeña*)

Air Seychelles Short 360. (*Air Seychelles*)

A Pacific Coastal Short 360. (*Pacific Coastal*)

In 2009 one of the authors carried out a survey of all the operators still using aircraft from the Skyvan/330/360 family. He was given considerable help by Dougie Corkhill of the Bombardier Belfast Customer Services which handled matters concerning Shorts' legacy aircraft. It was established that there were 223 of the aircraft still flying for 77 operators in North, Central and South America, Europe, Africa, Australia, the Middle East, the Sub-Continent, the Far East, the Caribbean, the Indian Ocean and the Pacific Ocean. He contacted all of these and received some very interesting responses from such diverse operators as: Air Cargo Carriers, Milwaukee, Wisconsin, which had a fleet of 25 330s and 360s, another freight company, Alliance Air Charter in Texas; hauling goods by Skyvan in the far north for Arctic Transportation Services in Alaska, in the Yukon, Northwest Territories and Nunavut for Summit Air and also in the Yukon for Rovic Air; cargo for mining companies in Congo with Swala Airlines; postal deliveries for Corporate Air in Hawaii and, closer to home, with Ben Air A/S of Denmark and Nightexpress in Germany. Scheduled passenger services were provided by Air Seychelles, Freedom Air, Guam (the largest and southernmost of the Mariana Islands in the Western Pacific), La Costeña in Nicaragua, Pacific Coastal Airlines of Vancouver and PT Deraya, Jakarta, Indonesia and Tiara Air in Aruba. Mixed passenger and cargo loads were carried by Trans Air Inc of Honolulu with seven 360s. More unusual tasks included electro-magnetic survey operations

Two US Forest Service C-23s. *(US Forest Service)*

A Fugro Skyvan in flight. *(Fugro Airborne Surveys)*

Tiara Air Short 360. *(Tiara Air)*

Smoke-jumpers in a US Forest Service C-23. *(US Forest Service)*

worldwide with Fugro Airborne Surveys of Western Australia, parachute training with CAE Aviation of Luxembourg, Pink Aviation Services, Vienna and Perris Valley Skydiving in Southern California and fire-fighting by parachuting in 'smoke-jumpers' from Sherpas with the US Forest Service. In November 2013 Dougie wrote to the authors, "Our records currently show there are 61 SD360 in operation – and 26 SD3-30, four of which are C-23B aircraft being operated by NASA and two by a company named Win Aviation. The C-23B and C-23B+ aircraft (37) in operation with the Army National Guard are currently in storage in different locations throughout the USA. The aircraft have not been withdrawn from service but are to be kept in a flyable condition while in storage [it is likely that they

will be advertised for disposal, indeed up to 15 have been allocated to the US Forest Service]. Skyvans are a nightmare, we never hear from any of the operators other than those operating in Europe but at a guess I would say around approximately 50." It was reported in December 2013 that two C-23s were at Prestwick en-route to the USA, having been retired from duty with the Multinational Force & Observers in Sinai, enforcing the 1979 Camp David Peace Accords between Egypt and Israel. The mission was two-fold: first to use the C-23 as an observation platform to monitor military activity on the Sinai to ensure compliance with the peace treaty between Israel and Egypt, and, second, to provide transportation to personnel and cargo from different locations throughout the region.

NASA C-23 pilot Rich Rogers at Fairbanks, Alaska. *(Rich Rogers)*

The spectacular Alaskan scenery viewed from the cockpit of a C-23. *(Rich Rogers)*

A C-23B in the hangar at the NASA Wallop's Flight Facility, Virginia in 2013. *(NASA Keith Koehler)*

NASA acquired four C-23B Sherpa aircraft in January 2012 from the US Army to be based at the Goddard Space Flight Center, Wallops Flight Facility in Virginia, on research duties. C-23 pilot, Rich Rogers, wrote to the authors, "The cabins of our four aircraft have been modified to upload various scientific instruments to fly the NASA CARVE mission. We have flown over 600 flight hours in the last two years mainly from May through October based in Fairbanks, Alaska. The mission name 'CARVE' is an acronym which stands for 'Carbon in Arctic Reservoirs Vulnerability Experiment', collecting detailed measurements of important greenhouse gases on local to regional scales in the Alaskan Arctic and demonstrates new remote sensing and improved modelling capabilities to quantify Arctic carbon fluxes and carbon cycle-climate processes. Ultimately, CARVE will provide an integrated set of data that will provide unprecedented experimental insights into Arctic carbon cycling. The Arctic-proven NASA C-23 Sherpa aircraft flies an innovative airborne remote sensing payload. It includes an L-band radiometer/radar and a nadir-viewing spectrometer to deliver the first simultaneous measurements of surface parameters that control gas emissions (ie, soil moisture, freeze/thaw state, surface temperature) and total atmospheric columns of carbon dioxide, methane, and carbon monoxide. The aircraft payload also includes a gas analyser that links greenhouse gas measurements directly to World Meteorological Organization standards. Flights occur during the spring, summer and early fall when Arctic carbon fluxes are large and change rapidly. Further, at these times, the sensitivities of ecosystems to external forces such as fire and anomalous variability of temperature and precipitation are maximised. Continuous ground-based measurements provide temporal and regional context as well as calibration for CARVE airborne measurements."

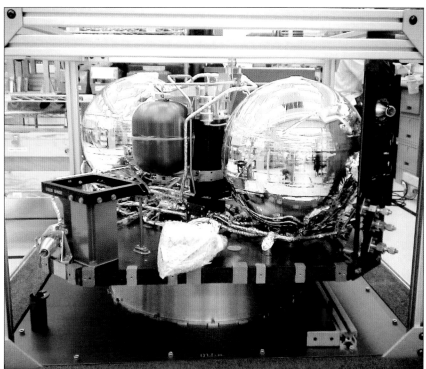

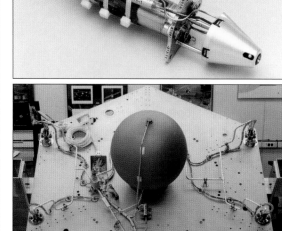

MR-103C Rocket Engine Assembly
(flying on Skynet-4). *(European Space Propulsion Ltd)*

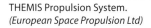

THEMIS Propulsion System.
(European Space Propulsion Ltd)

Earth Observing-1 Propulsion System.
(European Space Propulsion Ltd)

Northern Ireland's growing role in space propulsion: a recent international relationship between two large engineering organisations, which had its beginnings in April 2012, is well on its way to manufacturing key equipment for 'In Space' manoeuvring and control of space satellites. Aerojet Rocketdyne is the largest and most diversified rocket propulsion company in the US, and a worldwide leader in missile, launch vehicle and satellite propulsion systems. In addition to powering the GPS and Iridium satellite constellations, the company's products are orbiting Saturn, sitting on Mars and have just left the solar system on the Voyager spacecraft. After a long search throughout Europe for a suitable partner, Aerojet Rocketdyne has set up a wholly owned subsidiary – European Space Propulsion Ltd (ESP) based in Belfast and working closely with Thales Air Defence

to develop, manufacture and test 'In Space' propulsion devices for European customers. Thales leadership position in missile systems, highly engineered products requiring precision manufacturing, first rate quality systems and knowledge of working with US companies and governments was a perfect match for Aerojet Rocketdyne's plans for European expansion. The propulsion hardware to be built in Belfast covers a range of thrusters and complete systems including mono-propellant, bi-propellant and electric propulsion. ESP are currently working with a number European commercial and government customers to develop a comprehensive offering and look forward to the first Belfast manufactured propulsion equipment being used in space.

Built in Belfast, the forward fuselage, engine nacelles and horizontal stabiliser of the Global 5000 business jet. *(Bombardier Belfast)*

The C Series prototype lands after its maiden flight. *(Bombardier Belfast)*

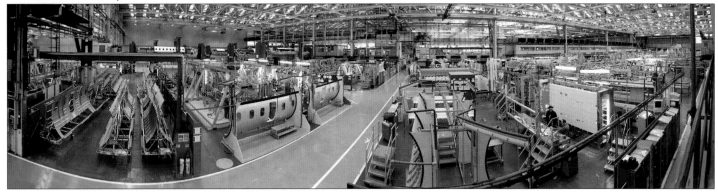

Inside the Bombardier Factory in Belfast. *(Bombardier Belfast)*

In November 2012 thousands of jobs were secured in Belfast when Vistajet, the business jet rental group, placed an order with Bombardier potentially worth $7.8 billion for 50 Global 5000 and Global 6000 and six of the forthcoming top-of-the-range Global 8000 (with an option for a further 86 of the Global high-speed, intercontinental business jet range). This represented the largest ever business aircraft sales in the Company's history. Some 900 from Bombardier's Belfast workforce of 5500 are committed to the Global 5000 and 6000 programmes, including the design, development and production of the forward fuselage, engine nacelles, horizontal stabiliser and other major composite parts. Belfast also plays a leading part in the C-Series 100–150 seat regional passenger jets, building fuselage section and wing components for this family of aircraft, which Bombardier is hoping will break the grip exerted by Boeing and Airbus on the short-haul sector of the market. It is being marketed as considerably more quiet and fuel efficient that the current generation of aircraft. Moreover, the complex, all-composite wings, which are being assembled on Queen's Island, incorporate a world-first resin infusion technology developed and patented in Belfast, where a new 600,000 square feet facility was opened by David Cameron on 11 October 2013. The first CS100, C-FBCS, completed its maiden flight from Montreal-Mirabel on 16 September 2013. Currently the order book stands at 177 firm orders plus more than 200 options.

Thompson Vantage XL business class seats *(Thompson Aero Seating)*

The factory site at Kilkeel. *(BE Aerospace)*

B/E Aerospace (UK) Ltd in Kilkeel manufactures seats for the airline industry worldwide and is located at the foot of the Mourne Mountains in Kilkeel. B/E Aerospace has its headquarters in the USA – a global organisation which is the leading provider of aircraft interior products for the commercial, business jet and military markets. The Kilkeel story began in the 1960s with investment from UK-based companies, local council representatives and businessmen bringing much needed employment and engineering skills to the town – Aircraft Furnishing Ltd was born. In those early days the Kilkeel plant was primarily involved in the manufacture of seat components and seat frame structures, which were shipped on a weekly basis to the parent company based near London, for final assembly. The Kilkeel plant became increasingly involved in the seat manufacture process, upholstery products began to be manufactured; the welded seat frame became redundant and it was replaced by lightweight aluminium machined components and modular design. In 1993 the company was acquired by B/E Aerospace and joined three other seat manufacturing companies who had previously been competitors and were all now part of the global group. Post the B/E acquisition Kilkeel's future was in question due to its size and location. Things turned around with the award of a large business class seat order for Japan Airlines; the first time they had chosen a supplier outside Japan. This order and

the performance from the Kilkeel team firmly set the plant up with the best in the business. In 2001, the decision was taken to close the PTC Aerospace plant in Connecticut and transfer its products to Kilkeel. This decision showed the level of confidence B/E had in Kilkeel. Several large investments have been made in recent years, including the opening of a new purpose-built assembly facility with office accommodation in 1999 and a further extension in 2006 with the purpose-built composite design and manufacture facility linked to assembly. Kilkeel continues to lead the way in innovative and lean techniques. Seat production methods are continually changing and improving to ensure efficiency and cost effectiveness. The Company employs over 800 people in Kilkeel. Established in 2001, Thompson Aero Seating, based in Portadown, County Armagh, designs, engineers, manufactures and assembles innovative premium seating solutions for commercial aircraft. Currently employing around 180 staff, and with extensive in-house manufacturing capabilities, Thompson's continues to grow with 115,000 sq ft of manufacturing capacity and further expansion planned. The current product range includes the Thompson Vantage, and Vantage XL business class seats and the Cozy Suite for the Economy and Premium Economy cabins, with major airline customers worldwide including Brussels Airlines, Air Canada, American Airlines and Qantas.

Denroy chairman, John Rainey and Flight Lieutenant Tom Bould with a Typhoon of No 1 (F) Squadron, RAF at Aldergrove on 21 March 2014. *(Denroy Plastics)*

ADS (AeroSpace Defence Security) is the Trade Organisation advancing UK aerospace, defence, security and space industries, with Farnborough International Limited as a wholly-owned subsidiary. Together with its regional partners, ADS represents over 2600 UK companies. ADS NI was established to advance these sectors in Northern Ireland. Launched at the Farnborough Airshow in July 2010, the organisation works closely with Invest NI to grow and ensure the continued success of these vital industries in Northern Ireland by bringing together leaders from the major aerospace, defence, security and space companies and the Universities to collectively set the direction for the industry. Its priorities are to help member companies develop, to increase market share and to raise awareness internationally of Northern Ireland's capability and technology. ADS NI currently has 61 member companies. ADS companies contribute around £900m to the Northern Ireland economy and support around 8000 high value jobs. The ADS NI office is hosted by Bombardier in Belfast. Members' logos are used to illustrate this page and underline the diversity of work undertaken. As an example, JW Kane describes its work as follows: "this precision engineering firm has been established since 1984 and currently supports a workforce of around 65 employees. We have a proven success rate of supply to many 'blue chip' customers within the aerospace industry. We are committed to excellence in product quality and in meeting customer specific requirements. Our modern, purpose-built facilities are equipped with leading edge machining technology. The main material used in our machining process is aluminium. As well as this, we machine steel, titanium, nylon, tufnol and also carbon fibre." Another member, Denroy Plastics of Bangor, a leading supplier of injection moulding services and associated assemblies to the aerospace and defence industries, celebrated in 2014 winning a £1,000,000 new contract to produce further components for the multi-role Eurofighter Typhoon. Denroy now supplies 180 separate parts for the Typhoon, the most plastic parts supplied by any single company in the world.